Stowe House Saving an Architectural Masterpiece

Edited by Nick Morris

STOWE HOUSE

Saving an Architectural Masterpiece

SCALA

First published in 2018 by
Scala Arts & Heritage Publishers Ltd
10 Lion Yard, Tremadoc Road, London SW4 7NQ, UK

www.scalapublishers.com

In association with
Stowe House Preservation Trust
Stowe. Buckingham MK18 5EH, UK

www.stowe.co.uk

ISBN 978-1-78551-111-0

Project manager and copy editor: Linda Schofield
Designed and typeset in Kingfisher by Dalrymple
Printed and bound in China

10 9 8 7 6 5 4 3 2 1

Frontispiece: The grandeur of Stowe House reflected in the Octagon Lake.

Front cover: The South Front of Stowe House with one of the Medici Lions.

Back cover: The glamour of the South Front at night.

Foreword

My first encounter with Stowe House came at an early and impressionable age, in 1967. I was a schoolboy at a nearby and very competitive school, and our team was at Stowe to take part in cross-country running. At one stage the course burst without warning onto the great South Front of the house and I was immediately stunned by its beauty, although even then it was clearly physically tired and partially supported by scaffolding. The sheer magnificence of the architecture and art momentarily took my breath away – not helpful for a cross-country runner – and I dawdled past in a state of admiration and wonderment. In so doing, I was overtaken by two Stoics, so the course was clearly designed to catch out prospective aesthetes like me, but the memory lingers to this day. A later visit as a 30-year-old to a charity dance in the Marble Saloon is seared into my memory by the sight of the floodlit Corinthian Arch 'floating' over the view from the Portico.

In 1996 I returned to Stowe in a more formal capacity as Chairman of the Historic Buildings Council (HBC), by then incorporated into English Heritage, and I led a team of experts and hugely experienced staff to look at the house and the challenges it presented. Again its magnificence was breathtaking even though its condition had visibly deteriorated in the meantime. On this occasion, however, I was free to linger with my group and stare, listen and learn, and I recall marvelling at the South Front as our experts talked about the house and its significance, and then scarily moved to the likely issues that must be addressed by any organisation attempting to save this artefact for posterity. I was all too aware of the finite funding available to the HBC, and the difficulties facing the National Trust (NT), which had taken on the gardens and temples in 1989. That was a wonderful start in preserving the whole, but the task of rescuing the house did seem all but insurmountable even though all of us on the HBC recognised without demur that it was one of the most important cultural monuments in Britain and somehow had to be salvaged at almost any cost.

Fortunately there were also many individuals who were keen to support the renovation of Stowe. Colin Amery, then Director of World Monuments Fund Britain, and friends at SAVE had been banging the drum for Stowe and demanding urgent action at least to halt the decline if not to restore and conserve. Richard Broyd had persuaded Dame Jennifer Jenkins at the NT to take on the gardens and he was now adding his hugely influential voice to the clamour that something 'must be done this time'. They and other fearless champions of heritage aligned with the School governors in an act of exemplary generosity to form the Stowe House Preservation Trust (SHPT) in 1997 and the story of the turnaround began.

To my surprise and delight, I was approached by the SHPT in 2006 through its then Chairman Sir Angus Stirling – one of the heroes of this story – to become the next Chairman of the SHPT.

In 2007 the task was still daunting but the early phases already achieved by the SHPT with Heritage Lottery Fund (HLF) support had proven just what could be done. By the time I took over, the North Front was restored as indeed was the front of the South Portico, and more tellingly the roofs over the central pavilion had gone from parlous temporary structures to spectacular leaded and slated faithful and highly skilful restorations. So the central section of the house was essentially safe and the great Marble Saloon had not only had its precipitous and dangerous water tanks removed and its roof renewed but it had also been sensitively conserved throughout. However, the scale of work that lay ahead of the SHPT continued to threaten the very survival of the house. The Library roof between the two pavilions was no more than a temporary structure of the 1950s with what was left of a felt cover on it. Instead of supporting the Library ceiling beneath it, it was actually bearing on the ancient timbers leading to cracking of the ceiling and visible distortions. A hideous safety net spanned underneath the magnificent plasterwork to protect the studious pupils below. At the western end of the house scaffolding right up to the top of the piano nobile was shoring up fragile but massive blocks of original decorative stonework and their linked architraves and lintels, and pathways were fenced off for fear that stones might fall onto unsuspecting victims. Had either of these disasters occurred and major structural failures ensued then the house would have had to be closed in large part for safety reasons alone. If the winter rains had come through the Library ceiling they would not only have destroyed much of the remaining plasterwork but would also have surged on down into Sir John Soane's Gothic Library, which was the Headmaster's nerve centre as he successfully rebuilt the School's academic and financial standing.

This fascinating book recounts in detail the work that has gone on over the last 18 years to bring the house into the condition in which we find it today. It has been a huge challenge, which has been supported by the extraordinary generosity of private individuals and grant-giving bodies, and by an unrelenting faith that we have all been given the task of rescuing this magnificent monument at whatever cost and effort. Key individuals have played vital parts too numerous to be mentioned, but do often star in the following chapters and to all of them I am indebted as is the Board of the SHPT.

The job is not yet finished but the structure of the building is very largely saved with skilfully restored roofs and several superbly conserved interiors. There is much still to do, but plans are advancing rapidly to complete the remaining tasks. What is perhaps most heartening is that over the last decade the SHPT has been able to move on from essential external fabric repairs, and full-blown renewal in some cases, to the more artistic and intellectually challenging refurbishment of priceless interiors, the replacement of statuary, conservation of ceilings and even as an ultimate sweetener the rediscovery of potentially great artwork in a wall painting covered over since around 1800. Work continues steadily, but the risks have been massively reduced and the highly visible renovation projects such as the Library ceiling and the State Music Room are very rewarding compared with the unseen but vital precursors like slate, render and downpipes. The journey has been challenging and has caused us some sleepless nights but the privilege of working on such a fine monument with a dedicated, skilful and unrelentingly optimistic group of colleagues and professionals has been the high spot of an entire career for a lover of world-class historic buildings.

ANDREW FANE
Chairman, Stowe House Preservation Trust

following pages The balustrade along the South Front with its copper urns.

Introduction

Since World Monuments Fund (WMF) was founded in 1965, it has been instrumental in advocating, guiding and providing financial support to rescue significant buildings across the globe deemed to be at risk from neglect, vandalism, armed conflict or natural disaster. In the case of Stowe House, the passage of time and its intensive use had taken their toll and so inclusion on WMF's biennial Watch List in 2002 and 2004 was a timely reminder that even the most careful of owners cannot always provide the level of upkeep that historic buildings demand. The Watch nomination acknowledged the work of Stowe School in maintaining Stowe House since 1923 but served to draw attention to the condition of this grand country house. The School had rescued the house from almost certain demolition in the 1920s and, in an inspired act of conservation, had gifted the gardens to the National Trust in 1989, but the work required to restore the building was beyond the means of the owners and, in 1998, Stowe House was placed on the English Heritage Register of Buildings at Risk. The formation of the Stowe House Preservation Trust (SHPT) in 1997 and the agreement of a six-phase restoration plan gave grounds for hope that WMF's involvement and that of its British affiliate could raise the profile of Stowe House and provide tangible support to the SHPT and Stowe School as they worked to deliver that restoration programme.

It would be hard to overstate the importance of Stowe House in terms of its architectural and artistic value or the contribution made by its owners to social history. Over two centuries, it was expanded and modified by some of Britain's most famous architects, among them Sir John Vanbrugh, James Gibbs, William Kent, Robert Adam, Thomas Pitt and Sir John Soane. Equally, it bears witness to the works of some of the greatest artists from Continental Europe. Vincenzo Valdrè, Giovanni Battista Borra, Francesco Sleter and Georges-François Blondel all left their mark on the house, while poets such as Thomas Addison and Alexander Pope and the art critic Horace Walpole wrote admiringly about the house and gardens. The Temple-Grenville family played a major role in the public life of the eighteenth century, producing four Prime Ministers and many government ministers whose acts influenced the course of the century. If Stowe's walls could talk, they might well recount political discussions that steered the country through this tumultuous period of history. Stowe's Watch Listing alongside places like the temples of Angkor Wat in Cambodia, Agra's Mughal gardens and the rock-cut churches in Ethiopia might give some idea of its significance on the worldwide architectural stage and its role as a political powerhouse.

Since 2002, WMF and WMF Britain have worked alongside the partners on site to bring Stowe House back to its former glory. With the generous help of the Robert W. Wilson Challenge to Preserve Our Heritage, the Paul Mellon Estate and many others, we have been instrumental in raising funds for the magnificent Marble Saloon, the restoration of the South Front and the State Room interiors, as well as the return of the Medici lions to the South Front. This has been a long but very satisfying process in which painstaking research, attention to detail and the application of skilled craftsmanship have all come together to produce the breathtaking results that we see today. Work on this outstanding place continues and we at WMF Britain are proud of our association with the project that is recorded in this book.

JOHN DARLINGTON
Executive Director, WMF Britain

opposite One of the Medici lions overlooking the landscape garden.

Chapter One

The Significance of the 'superb mansion at Stowe'

JEREMY MUSSON

The North Front of Stowe today: the house has always been the centrepiece of the landscape garden and its constellation of temples and statues.

Stowe House is the crafted, layered centrepiece of a landscape garden of international repute from the early eighteenth century. It has in some ways been an elusive character in modern British architectural historical studies, and surprisingly overlooked in many standard architectural histories.[1] The stimulation of research by George Clarke, Michael Gibbon, Michael Bevington and others, especially that which preceded the recent campaign of conservation and restoration carried out by the Stowe House Preservation Trust since 1997, has brought it back to wider attention.[2]

New ideas have flowed from the restoration of the most significant interiors, paralleled with work by the National Trust (NT) in the landscape garden since 1989.[3] All this knowledge and activity has naturally helped to reveal again the identity and significance of Stowe House. One anonymous 1769 visitor observed, 'if any house can claim the epithet of magnificence, it must be this'.[4] Lord Shelburne, the well-travelled connoisseur and patron of Robert Adam and no admirer of Lord Temple, nonetheless wrote of him, 'He was magnificent in his buildings ... rendering Stowe one of the finest private palaces in Europe'.[5] Thus anyone wishing to understand how 'magnificence' was achieved in the eighteenth century must study Stowe.

Many significant designers contributed to its eighteenth-century development. As John Phibbs recently observed, 'It is not possible to overestimate the importance of Stowe to [Capability] Brown and to the whole English landscape movement'.[6] It was, he argues, 'the cradle of experiment' for Sir John Vanbrugh, James Gibbs, William Kent, Charles Bridgeman and Brown himself, who was appointed Head Gardener at Stowe in 1741. Nor was this sense of inventive activity in the garden alone, for Vanbrugh and Kent, and then later Georges-François Blondel, Giovanni Battista Borra, Vincenzo Valdrè, Robert Adam, Thomas Pitt (Lord Camelford) and Sir John Soane, all contributed to the studied magnificence of the mansion house. Few country houses in England can claim such an encyclopedic – and international – architectural pedigree.

By the early nineteenth century, Stowe House had undoubtedly become one of the greatest country houses in England: in scale, splendour and setting. It was a house forged by dynastic ambition, shaped and sharpened by money, travel, politics and classical ideals. The creation, of both house and garden, took place over two principal periods in the eighteenth century, and under the direction of two shrewd and sophisticated patrons, Sir Richard Temple, created

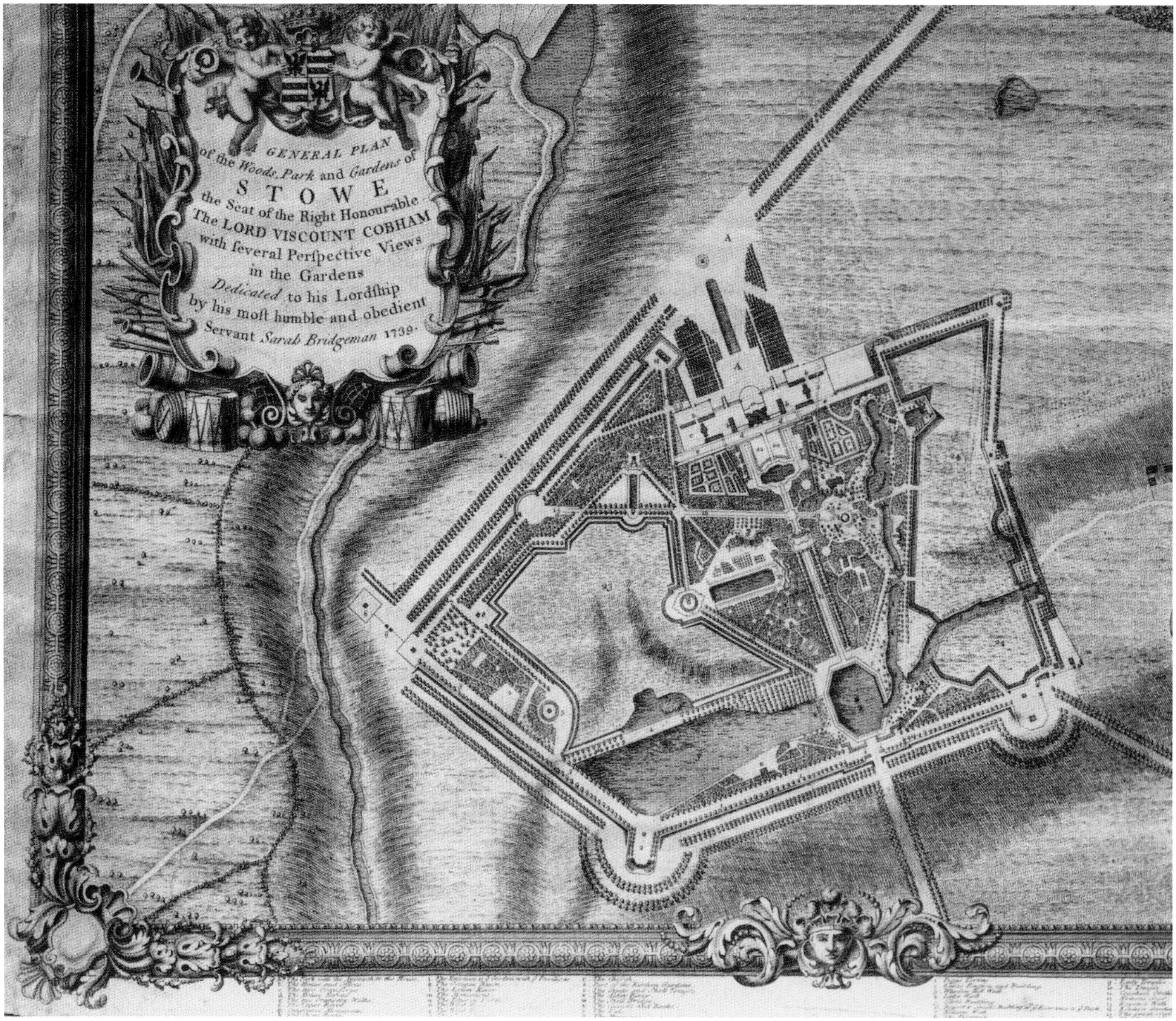

Detail of a survey plan of the Stowe estate, drawn by Charles Bridgeman and published by Sarah Bridgeman in 1739 (see also p. 122).

1st Viscount Cobham in 1718, and his nephew and heir, Richard Grenville, 2nd Earl Temple, an able architectural draughtsman, who directed some of the improvements to the garden himself. His nephew, created 1st Marquess of Buckingham, completed the decoration of the great State Rooms and his own son, who was later made the 1st Duke of Buckingham and Chandos, was a renowned collector and patron of Soane, who designed the Gothic Library at Stowe (with its ceiling decoration incorporating the 726 armorial quarterings of the family).[7]

John Beckett notes how the Temple-Grenvilles provide 'virtually a textbook example of how to achieve promotion',[8] through landownership, marriages that brought wealth and careers in politics: the Grenville family produced two Prime Ministers in the eighteenth and early nineteenth centuries, and was related by marriage to both William Pitt the Elder and William Pitt the Younger.[9]

Magnificence was also a feature of function. The mansion house – like most major country houses – was as much a machine for socialising as a political house per se. In 1750, Stowe was already said to possess 'some of the finest Rooms perhaps in Europe' and in the 1770s and 1780s the principal rooms were refashioned intensively at the forefront of neoclassical taste.[10] These richly decorated spaces were contrived for elegant display and use, settings for music and dining, conversation and pleasing idleness: in 1848, it was commented that 'Stowe has, perhaps, been more frequently the scene of royal hospitality than any other aristocratic residence in England'.[11] The ambition, since the time of Lord Cobham, had been, as Beckett has observed, 'to make Stowe a house suitable for an aristocrat of the highest rank'.[12]

Entertainments at Stowe naturally involved both house and garden temples, and almost constant interaction between the two. Horace Walpole memorably described a visit with the Princess Amelia, second daughter of George II, in July 1770, which emphasises this sense of movement between house, landscape and park buildings:

We breakfasted at half an hour after nine; but the Princess did not appear till it was finished; then we walked in the garden or drove about it in cabriolets, till it was time to dress: dined at three ... and then again into the garden till past seven, when we came in, drank tea and coffee, and played at Pharoah till ten, when the Princess retired, and we went to supper, and before twelve to bed ... the number of buildings and variety of scenes in the garden made each day different from the rest.[13]

There is also an unusual record of the memories of a female servant regarding one of the dinners:

nothing can exceed the grandeur and order by which everything was conducted. Twelve gentlemen well-dressed waited at table, twenty-four in livery waited in the next room, and in the grand hall, near the dining room was a grand concert of music ... I never saw any entertainment conducted with more care, order, and decorum.[14]

Lady Mary Coke described the same visit, commenting on how much had changed in recent years, 'So many years & so many alterations since I was here, makes it quite a new place to me', and mentioning how much she admired the hosts, 'Nobody can do the honours of their House with more ease & propriety than Ld & Ly Temple'.[15] She too recorded the pleasing circuits of the temples, and recalled the evening of 3 July, 'At night part of the Elysian fields were lighted up & we supped in the Grotto: the gardens were filled with people'.[16] Walpole and Coke both clearly admired the park for its glamour and amenity; nearly 20 years before, in 1751, Walpole remarked to a friend, 'I do like that Albano glut of buildings, let them be ever so much condemned.'[17] In between those two visits, Earl Temple had initiated considerable simplifications and alterations, which included the resiting and removal of some buildings in the interests of a grander spectacle.

From the 1720s people had filled the park; indeed international visitors responded to it with awe and wonder, and from these decades Stowe's best qualities were imitated in their native lands.[18] The role of the house in the park was that of the linchpin of the messages and monuments of Stowe's landscape. Indeed, such a landscape with its constellation of

Benton Seeley's 1762 guidebook about Stowe, one of a selection on display in the Discovery Centre.

structures and views would have made no sense to a contemporary, without a mansion at its core. This centrality is illustrated by examples of the guidebook promoted by Benton Seeley. First published in 1744, it passed through 17 editions by 1797, gradually adding more and more about the house – especially in the 1770s and 1780s – so that by 1788 substantial descriptions of the architectural interiors and contents had been included.[19]

To compare two examples: the 1749 version is entitled *A description of the Gardens of Lord Viscount Cobham, at Stow* [sic] *in Buckinghamshire.*[20] Images of the temples and monuments in the gardens predominate but this guide also (for the first time) includes illustrations of the South and North Fronts, drawn by Seeley and engraved by George Vertue, on a page to be folded outwards as if no book could quite contain their stately dimensions. Even so, there is no text about the house itself, this not appearing until the 1759 edition.[21]

By 1788, the guidebook has a full account of the house, including not only the pull-out illustrations of the north and south elevations, but also a floor plan of the piano nobile (first introduced in 1763); the title was by now extended to read: *Stowe: a description of the house and gardens of the most noble and puissant prince, George Grenville Nugent Temple, Marquis of Buckingham, Earl Temple, Viscount and Baron Cobham: A New edition with all the Alterations and Improvements which have been made ther[e]in, to the present Time … Embellished with a General Plan of the Gardens, and also a separate Plan of the House, and each Building, with Perspective Views of the Same.*[22] The illustrations of the many temples provided a source of ready reference for the imitation of the same buildings elsewhere.[23]

To fully understand Stowe, it is also important to recognise that Stowe House was one of the eighteenth-century powerhouses of England and in effect the nursery of a political class (Lord Cobham's young protégés were dubbed 'Cobham's cubs').[24] As John Martin Robinson has noted, 'Stowe was one of the half dozen principal seats of the Whig aristocracy, and its owners, the Temple-Grenvilles, were a dominant force in the political life of the country'.[25] Several other

The South Front today.

great houses (such as Althorp, in Northamptonshire) were hotbeds of Whig debate and intrigue, and through that helped shape the destiny and character of the nation and the way the nation engaged with the world, but few were set in parks that so visibly glittered with references to the politics of liberty and constitutional rule (and the poetry of Alexander Pope). Even more unusual was the very persistence of the design and creation of evocative and associative buildings throughout the eighteenth century.[26]

The initial refashioning of the 1670s' house by 1st Viscount Cobham (begun during a period of temporary disgrace in 1710–14 until his rehabilitation after the accession of George I) was a demonstration of both his culture and his dynastic ambition.[27] Lord Cobham's military and political career, his commitment to martial honour, his marriage to a wealthy brewing heiress, Anne Halsey, and his continuing hope for his family's increasing status, all helped to shape the early eighteenth-century Stowe. Indeed, it could be argued that he set the whole Stowe juggernaut in motion, establishing an estate and seat that put his family (in this case the Grenville nephew and his heirs) on the path to the highest honours of nobility in the land: eventually earning a dukedom and four generations of Knights of the Garter. Given his own regiment in 1702 by William III, Lord Cobham was appointed Major-General in 1709 and Lieutenant-General in 1710.[28]

So did Stowe perhaps grow at first in the shadow of the architectural grandeur of that great mansion at nearby Blenheim, in Oxfordshire, designed as a house for a national hero and a monument to the victories of the age, and a man who had risen from gentry to Duke in one glorious lifetime? The references to martial honour, victory and fame are unavoidable at Stowe, although the house does not share Blenheim's overt martial symbolism in the iconography of the architecture. Blenheim's designer, Sir John Vanbrugh, former army officer and playwright-turned-architect (ably assisted in designing the house by Nicholas Hawksmoor), played an important part in laying out the original park at Blenheim; and from 1705, with Henry Wise, the Royal Gardener. Vanbrugh's intended plan was engraved for Volume III of *Vitruvius Britannicus* (1725).[29] Thomas Hearne considered the gardens of Blenheim 'very extraordinary and to exceed anything of that nature in England'.[30]

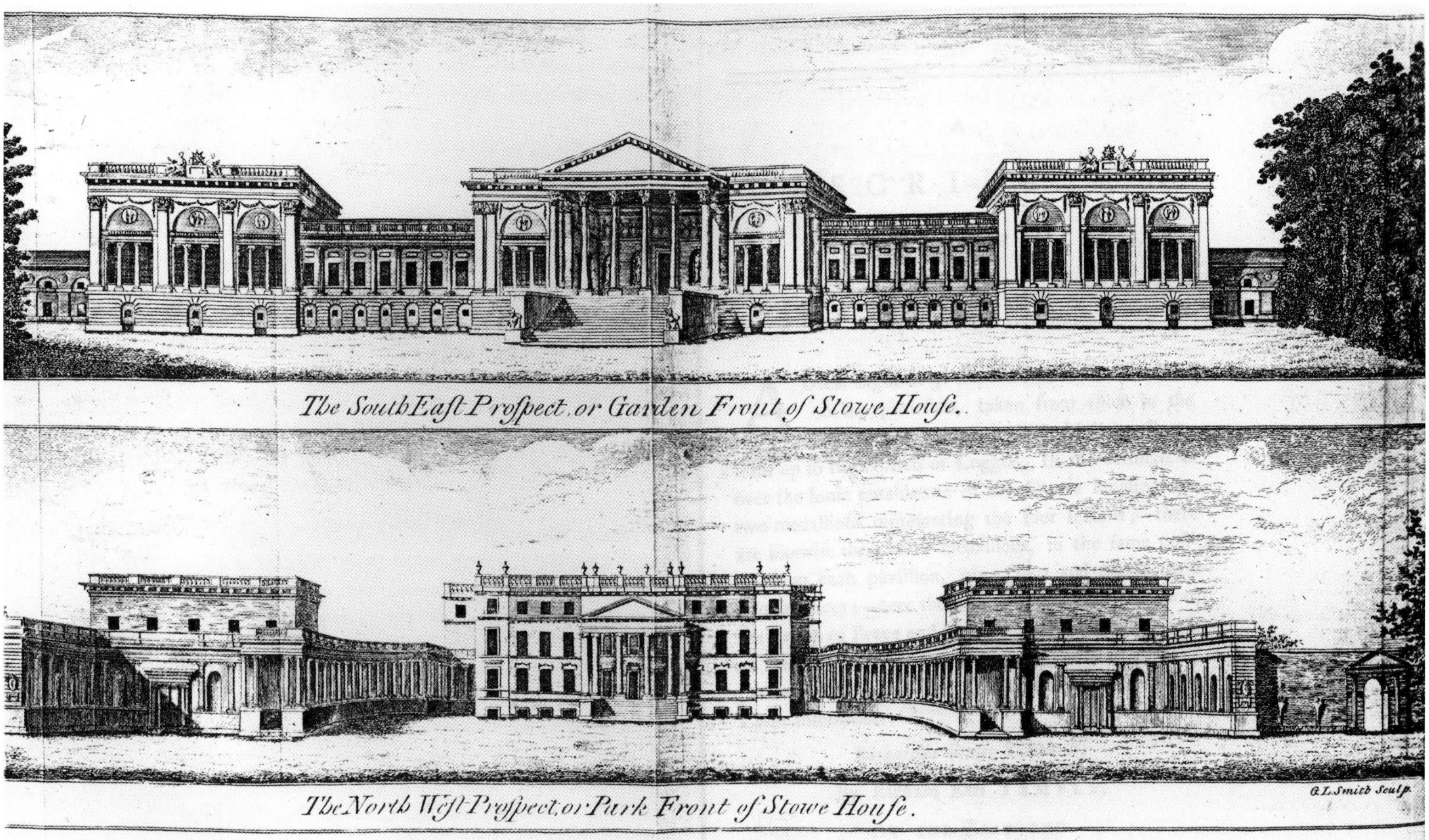

The South and North Fronts of Stowe from Benton Seeley's 1768 guidebook.

At Blenheim, Vanbrugh also first articulated his philosophy of the evocative and associative qualities of buildings (namely in his attempt in 1710 to preserve the remains of the old manor) referencing how that building could 'move more lively and pleasing Reflections on the Persons who have Inhabited them, on the Remarkable things that have been transacted in them; Or the extraordinary Occasions of Erecting Them'.[31] Abruptly dismissed from Blenheim by the Duchess of Marlborough in 1716, Vanbrugh had, by 1719 if not before, become involved in the house and garden (with Charles Bridgeman) at Stowe.[32]

Vanbrugh loved it. He wrote to his friend Jacob Tonson in July 1719, 'I lately went to my Ld Cobham a Visit to Stowe, where he is very well, and in very good humour; and much entertain'd with (besides his Wife) the Improvements of his House and Gardens, in which he Spends all he has to spare'.[33] Vanbrugh is the presumed designer of the grand Portico entrance to the North Front, with its slender Giant Order Ionic columns, which was added to the 13-bay late seventeenth-century house around 1720, probably to celebrate Cobham's ennoblement in 1714.[34]

As Vaughan Hart has pointed out, Vanbrugh, the brilliant dramatist, helped Cobham to make Stowe's landscape, among other things, 'the celebration of love between Cobham and his wife'. In 1720 the park had Vanbrugh's Rotunda, with a figure of Venus, as the apparent focus. Vanbrugh enjoyed his association with Stowe very much, writing to a friend in 1725 that 'we Stay'd at Stowe a Fortnight, a Place now so Agreeable that I had much ado to leave it at all'.[35]

Three decades later, Horace Walpole still recognised clearly the evocative, literary and theatrical character of Stowe's landscape and buildings (first fostered by Vanbrugh) in an account of his 1770 visit:

Every acre brings to one's mind some instance of parts or pedantry, of the taste or want of taste, of the ambition, or love of fame, or greatness, or miscarriages of those that have inhabited, decorated, planned or visited the place. Pope, Congreve, Vanbrugh, Kent, Gibbs, Lord Cobham, Lord Chesterfield, the mob of nephews, the Lytteltons, Granvilles, Wests, Leonidas Glover, and Wilkes, the late Prince of Wales, the King of Denmark, Princess Amelia, and the proud monuments of Lord Chatham's, now enshrined here, now anathemized there ... all these images crowd upon one's memory, and add visionary personages to the charming scenes.[36]

An echo of Blenheim is perhaps found too in the ceiling of the North Hall. Painted in grisaille on a faux gold mosaic background by William Kent in the early 1730s, it shows Cobham (seated) being presented with a sword by Mars, the god of war.[37] This was a reference to his first military commission in 1702, with King William III shown looking on from a portrait medallion, and is thought to be an iconographic programme suggested by the patron himself. Is this ceiling a homage to Sir James Thornhill's magnificent ceiling in the entrance hall of Blenheim, celebrating in allegory the successes of John Churchill (1st Duke of Marlborough), who, in the character of Mars, approaches Britannia (in the figure of Queen Anne) as mistress of the world?[38]

above left A 1763 engraving of the North Front of Blenheim House (Blenheim Palace), Oxfordshire.

above right Sir John Vanbrugh, by Sir Godfrey Kneller, *c.*1705.

opposite The North Hall ceiling at Stowe, with Viscount Cobham seated and receiving a sword from Mars, god of war, and King William III looking on from a portrait medallion held by two putti.

The breathtaking Marble Saloon's elliptical domed roof, built in the 1770s, was partly inspired by the circular domed roof of the Pantheon in Rome.

It often seems puzzling to modern eyes to find so many architects and designers at work at Stowe. Lord Cobham and his nephew the 2nd Earl Temple (and his nephew, created the 1st Marquess of Buckingham in 1784) were as lively in their exercise of patronage as they were in their lobbying for honours, always pressing for the best. Many leading architects were drawn into the unfolding iterations of the great gardens and house. Lord Cobham's architects were the most skilful British practitioners at the time; Earl Temple, by contrast, invited a series of Continental architects to contribute to the evolution of the house.[39]

Richard Temple, 1st Viscount Cobham, by Jean-Baptiste van Loo, *c.*1740.

The enrichment and remodelling of Stowe House in the 1770s and 1780s, especially the South Front and the key State Rooms – including the breathtaking oval Marble Saloon with its coffered ceiling and stuccoed frieze of a classical triumphal procession – made it one of the fullest expressions of a neoclassical country house in England. As Michael McCarthy observed, it had become 'the largest and most completely realised private neo-classical building in the world'.[40] By these various means, Stowe might be said finally to have exceeded in architectural impact Vanbrugh and Hawksmoor's triumphal palace at Blenheim.

The 1770s' works at Stowe included the addition of the sweeping colonnades, with their strong Roman character, to the North Front; these are not firmly attributed to any designer. Stowe entered a second phase of inventive recreation under Cobham's heir, Richard Grenville (who became 2nd Earl Temple on his mother's death in 1752), who also extended and naturalised the gardens, resiting or removing some of the earlier structures and making the landscape of Stowe as we know it today. The rebuilding of the South Front of the house was clearly a bid for architectural presence in the park, and in national

far left Richard Grenville, 2nd Earl Temple, by Robert Edge Pine, *c.*1776.

left George Grenville, 1st Marquess of Buckingham, by John Jackson, *c.*1812.

Robert Adam's 1771 design for the South Front of Stowe.

reputation. Lord Temple had first explored the idea with Borra in the 1750s, and yet more ambitiously with Blondel from the 1760s, but neither of their plans was executed.[41] Lord Temple then approached Robert Adam, who had spent a period in Rome in the 1750s and studied with Giovanni Battista Piranesi and Charles-Louis Clérisseau, and who had surveyed the ruined palace of Diocletian in Split (published 1764).[42]

Adam drew up a design in 1771, which appears to have set the profile and overall disposition of this remodelling, although his design was not executed exactly; there are also references to 'a famous Italian' being involved. It seems that Adam's design was taken in hand and simplified by Temple's younger cousin, Thomas Pitt (Lord Camelford), a talented amateur architect, who is the known designer of the great 1765 Corinthian Arch that frames the approach from the south. The remodelling of the South Front was finished by 1779. In 1827, James Dallaway wrote that 'T. Pitt ... was the sole designer of the superb mansion at Stowe',[43] but this can only have been true of the South Front, and Adam should be given some credit for that too (how he would have relished the chance to take control of the whole project at Stowe). Pitt's Corinthian Arch indicates the increasing visual significance of the mansion house.

In 1785, Walpole wrote to a friend, Henry Seymour Conway, of how 'I have often and often studied the new plan of Stowe; it is pompous', but he also added how the park buildings 'enrich that insipid country' and noted of the ensemble, 'the vastness pleases me more than I can defend'.[44] There can be little doubt that the very scale of Stowe's South Front stands out among the most ambitious country houses of the eighteenth century, closer in spirit to the Palladian Holkham Hall in Norfolk (from 1734) in the extensive spread of its south elevation, central portico and pavilions, or to the stately Wanstead in Essex, completed in 1722, or Wentworth Woodhouse in Yorkshire built in two major phases, 1725–34 and 1734–60, although

above Holkham Hall, Norfolk.

right Heveningham Hall, Suffolk, the Seat of Sir Gerrard Vanneck Bart, pen and ink and watercolour on paper, by Thomas van der Wilt, eighteenth century.

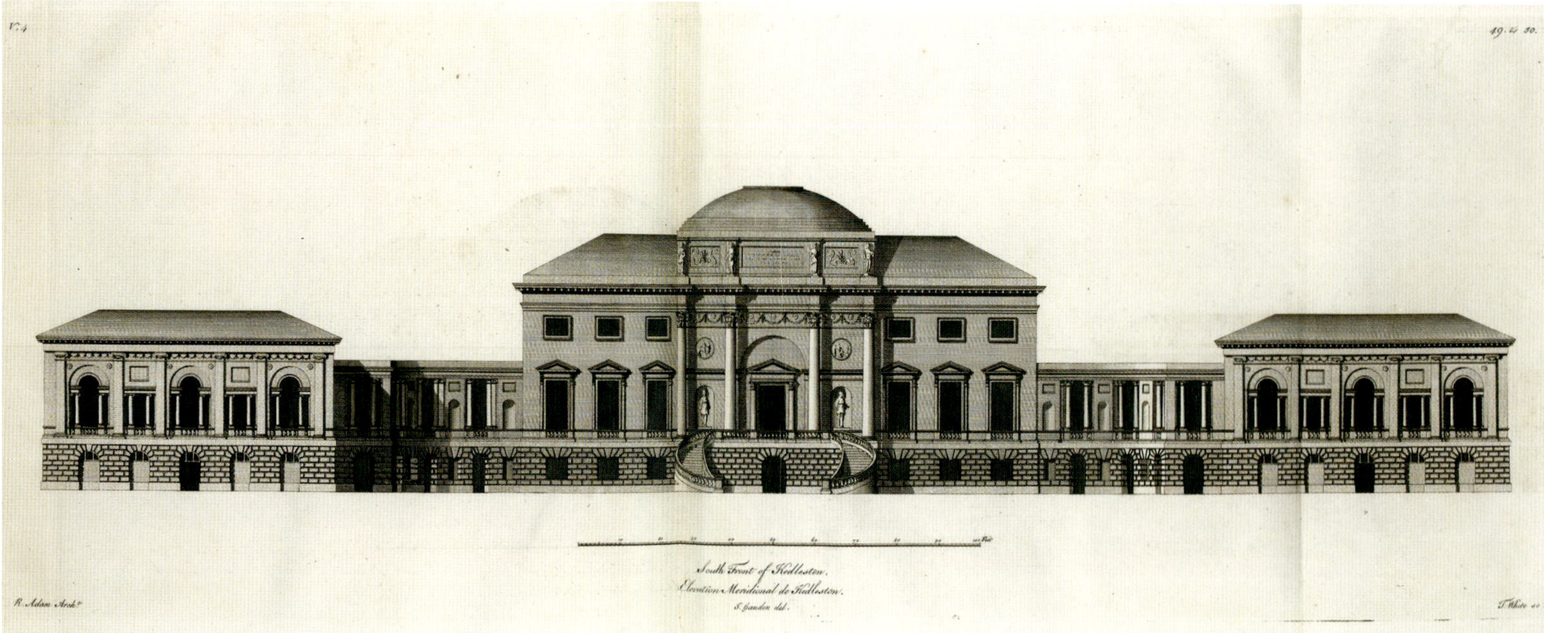

Stowe as rebuilt in the 1770s appears to have a longer elevation than the latter.[45] Sir Robert Taylor's Heveningham Hall, in Suffolk, of 1778–80, speaks of a similar bid for greatness of effect but has neither the elevated Portico nor the extent of Stowe.[46]

Perhaps the closest contemporary British work in terms of scale, neoclassical character and extent might be one of Robert Adam's own masterpieces, namely the south front of Kedleston Hall, as designed by Adam with the two projecting wings connected by curved corridors, but the wings were never executed.[47] Walpole was conscious of the scale of Stowe, and complained to a friend, Henry Seymour Conway, in 1770, that 'there is no sallying out of the house without descending a flight of steps as high as St Paul's'.[48]

The exterior stateliness of this new manifestation of Stowe was matched within. The great rooms of the main house along the South Front were remodelled in neoclassical taste, including the Marble Saloon, with the State Music Room and State Drawing Room (the latter now known as the Temple Room) either side, and the State Apartments. Work on the State Rooms and decoration appears to have continued into the 1780s, completed by the 1st Marquess, who had made the Grand Tour with Lord Bulkeley, and travelled in Rome, Naples and Pompeii in the mid-1770s.[49] The State Drawing Room and the State Music Room, as completed, expressed a decorative brilliance at the very height of fashion, reflecting tastes cultivated on the Grand Tour and remaining a marvel today.

above Robert Adam's dramatic design for the *South Front of Kedleston*, in John Woolfe and James Gandon, *Vitruvius Britannicus*, vol. IV (1767), plates 49–50; the quadrants and linked pavilions were not executed.

below Kedleston Hall, Derbyshire, today.

opposite Stowe's neoclassical enfilade from the Blue Room through the Library and beyond.

Decorative detail in the State Music Room: gilded frieze (*above*), musical emblems over the niche (*centre*) and Vincenzo Valdrè's playful take on putti (*below*).

The State Music Room was decorated in the Pompeian taste by Valdrè, in a brilliant play on the theme of temples: delicately painted figures, structures and grotesque motifs seem suspended against the pale ground colour. Valdrè's *Dance of the Hours* ceiling roundel was inspired directly by Guido Reni's famous ceiling in Rome, *Apollo and the Hours*.[50] The State Drawing Room (on the other side of the Marble Saloon) has an identical plan, and a plasterwork ceiling with attenuated classical figures, probably designed by Valdrè and executed by James Lovell.[51] Hung for many years in a rich orange-red damask, it was painted by Joseph Nash for the young Queen Victoria's album, after her visit in 1845, representing the room at its finest and most richly furnished, just three years before the 2nd Duke's virtual bankruptcy led to a major sale of the contents for 40 days in 1848 (see p. 56).[52] To the west of the State Drawing Room lay the Statue Gallery, which in 1817 became the State Dining Room, and to the east of the State Music Room was the 1790s' Library (previously a ballroom).

From the 1770s, these richly finished interiors were part of a bid for yet further social and artistic supremacy, all of which was by necessity acted out in front of a well-established audience. Stowe was already internationally famous, and from the 1740s it had become one of the most visited great estates in England (part of a fashionable circuit for travellers that included Blenheim, and Stourhead in Wiltshire). The ensemble of architecture and landscape, and its poetic and – for some – political associations (with ideals of liberty and constitutional government), influenced the designs of parks across Europe and beyond, from France to the German princely states, to Sweden and Russia.

In 1786, Stowe was visited by John Adams and Thomas Jefferson, subsequently the second and third presidents of the United States respectively. Adams described Stowe (grouped along with Hagley, in Worcestershire, and Blenheim) as 'superb', mentioning how he and Jefferson had explored all the buildings with interest, and that 'architecture, painting, statuary and poetry are all employed in those embellishments of these residences of greatness and luxury'.[53] Jefferson noted the alterations going on, and recorded the numbers of gardeners employed: '15. men and 18. boys employed in keeping pleasure grounds'.[54] He owned at least two copies of the Seeley guidebooks of Stowe, had a strong interest in classical architecture and garden design, and took inspiration from Stowe, Stourhead and elsewhere to his gardens and house at Monticello.[55]

Contemporary French landscape design was also influenced by great English landscaped gardens (*jardins anglais*), and by the theories and writings of Jean-Jacques Rousseau, who had visited Stowe in 1761: 'it is composed of very beautiful and very picturesque spots chosen to represent different kinds of scenery ... the master and creator of this superb domain has also erected ruins, temples and ancient buildings and they, like the scenes, exhibit a magnificence which is more than human'.[56]

One of the Continental gardens most linked to the example of Stowe (along with Claremont in Surrey

Monticello, the home of US President Thomas Jefferson, 1819.

The Temple of Venus at the English Grounds of Wörlitz, Germany.

and Stourhead) was that formed at Wörlitz by Prince Leopold III, Friedrich Franz of Anhalt-Dessau.[57] Prince Leopold's architect, Friedrich Wilhelm Von Erdmannsdorff, travelled with him to Britain in 1763–64 and recorded his impressions of Stowe House and gardens in brief:

the gardens there are very extensive, having a circumference of five miles. They are full of temples, pavilions, obelisks, pyramids and all kinds of monuments that would require an entire brochure to describe ... the ensemble seems over ornate to me. The house is very spacious and well furnished.[58]

Prince Leopold drew actively on the model of the landscapes and temples of Claremont, Stourhead and Stowe: for instance, his pivotal Temple of Venus was closely modelled on the Rotunda by Vanbrugh (as altered by Borra) at Stowe.[59]

Stowe was also one of the important sources for the parks and palaces commissioned by Catherine the Great: the park at Tsarskoye Selo (which has been described by Peter Hayden as 'The Russian Stowe'), the English Park for the 'English Palace' of Peterhof (the park designed by James Meaders who was brought out to Russia, and the palace and its grand pavilions by Giacomo Quarenghi), and finally Pavlovsk, perhaps the greatest blending of the English landscaped park style and neoclassical architecture in the Russian Empire.[60] Catherine the Great's admiration for Stowe is nowhere better expressed than in the famous 'Green Frog' creamware service of English parks and gardens that she commissioned from Wedgwood in 1773–74, which included 48 different scenes of Stowe on the dinner service.[61] The views of temples and vistas and the North Front were taken from engravings by George Bickham while the South Front curiously illustrated the ambitious, but never executed, proposal drawn up by Borra in the 1750s.[62]

The political careers of the Temple-Grenvilles, the ambition of the house and park, the extensive estates (at their greatest some 28,000 hectares), and the image of wealth and security all played their part in helping the family achieve the coveted rank of Marquess, then, in 1822, Duke; but the family's

far left Catherine II, Empress of Russia, walking in the Park at Tsarskoye Selo, oil on canvas, by Vladimir L. Borovikovsky, 1794.

left The 'Green Frog' dinner service made by Wedgwood, with a view of one of the proposed designs for Stowe's South Front (black and white detail).

left below The Palladian Bridge at Tsarskoye Selo.

The Rotunda at Stowe, by Sir John Vanbrugh, 1720–21, as altered by Borra.

fortunes perhaps never recovered from the draining expense of their building projects. The 2nd Duke had already narrowly escaped bankruptcy when he persuaded Queen Victoria and Prince Albert to stay in 1845, en route to Chatsworth. Most rooms appear to have been refurnished and redecorated for the event, and the house was undoubtedly seen in its full glory; Benjamin Disraeli called the visit 'a brilliant success', and the Queen was reported as saying 'I am sure I have no such splendid apartments in either of my palaces'.[63] By 1847, the 2nd Duke was almost entirely bankrupt, and most of the important contents of the house were sold in 1848.

His son, the 3rd Duke, managed to rescue the house and around 4,000 hectares, but when he died in 1889, the estate was inherited by a daughter, Lady Kinloss.[64] Lady Kinloss's son was killed in the First World War, and the estate was put up for sale by his younger brother, the Reverend Luis Grenville, in 1921. One Harry Shaw acquired it with a view to presenting the house to the nation, but it was sold again in 1922 and became the premises for a new public school. Thus the house and gardens were saved from threatened demolition, and were adapted for the School by Clough Williams-Ellis and others.[65] As mentioned above, the building is now vested in a charitable trust dedicated to its restoration and well-managed public opening. The School remains as the tenant, giving the building valuable continuing purpose and identity, while in 1989 the landscape park was given to the NT, the best guardian of such an important site.

The chapters that follow reveal the extraordinary progress that has been made in the restoration of Stowe House. This work (costing £40 million with grants from the Heritage Lottery Fund, World Monuments Fund, Country Houses Foundation and many others) has been based on rigorous research, involving complex but clearly reasoned decisions. In the main, the surviving interiors have been restored to their condition in the early years of the nineteenth century, with the majority of the principal rooms as they were in the late eighteenth century.[66] Just as Lord Cobham, and then Lord Temple, assembled some of the most talented designers of their age, so has the SHPT, working closely with its tenant, Stowe School, gathered and employed the skills and expertise of the best architects, conservators, curators, furniture-makers and experts on paint and textiles.[67] Through these means the great neoclassical mansion house at Stowe has, in effect, been rediscovered, and made 'a temple amongst temples' once more.

In perfect harmony, classical figures flank the view from the Marble Saloon to the landscape garden, with the Corinthian Arch on the horizon.

Chapter Two

The Architectural Development of Stowe House

MICHAEL BEVINGTON

The view from the South Portico across the Octagon Lake to the Corinthian Arch.

Today Stowe House and its landscape appear to be an architectural unity. The magnificent South Front gazing serenely towards the Corinthian Arch, the grand Portico of the North Front facing the equestrian statue of George I and the interior's enfilade of State Rooms all seem designed as a single ensemble. Yet none of these elements was conceived and completed as a unified whole, but took over a century to finish.

Four generations of the Temple and Grenville families shared a passion for architecture. Sir Richard Temple built the original house; Lord Cobham, Earl Temple and the Marquess of Buckingham altered and extended it. During the eighteenth and nineteenth centuries nine architects and designers worked on the house. Many were persuaded to contribute additional structures to the garden and park while they were involved in the mansion. Others provided plans and advice, including nine more architects and three of the owners.

The architectural development of Stowe House is significant not just for its sheer scale and complexity, but for the importance of some of its detailed elements. These include its original corner pavilion design, its remodelling as a classic Vanbrugh house, its groundbreaking neoclassical Garter Room, its unique Marble Saloon and State Music Room, its classical South Front, and its hidden gems of the Egyptian Hall and the Gothic Library.

Shortage of money helped preserve the eighteenth-century house and, since 1997, the Stowe House Preservation Trust (SHPT) has been managing the magnificent restoration of the exterior and the State Rooms.

The families' other interests included fine art, lavish entertainment, military service and politics. They could claim four Prime Ministers within some 50 years who helped Britain gain an empire, lose its American colonies, defeat the Napoleonic naval threat and see the final abolition of the slave trade.[1]

Sources include thousands of documents, mostly in the Huntington Library, California.[2] There are also engravings, drawings and photographs, along with a series of descriptions recording individual rooms from 1759 to 1838, sale catalogues from 1848, 1921 and 1922, and inventories from 1697, 1839 and 1871,[3] in addition to visitor accounts.[4] Building on existing literature,[5] this chapter seeks to elucidate the four main stages in the architectural development of Stowe House, in particular aiming to throw new light on the two phases of construction under Lord Cobham.

LONDON FASHION: SIR RICHARD TEMPLE, 3RD BARONET, 1677–1697

In 1653 Sir Richard Temple, the 3rd Baronet of Stowe, then aged 19, inherited the old Stowe house, along with £20,000 of debts. He paid these off mainly by land sales in 1656 and then reclaimed the Burton Dassett estate from his half-sister, Lady Baltinglass. By keeping the support of the 12 burgesses of Buckingham, who elected two MPs, he remained an MP for nearly 40 years and in 1672 was appointed a Commissioner of the Customs at a salary of £2,000. In 1675, aged 41, he married Mary Knapp, who had a fortune of £4,000. So by 1676 he had the means to commission a new house with a final cost of £5,030.[6] Its location was just below the ridge of a hill, facing the spire of the old parish church in Buckingham.

After the Great Fire of London in 1666 leading architects such as Sir Christopher Wren and Robert Hooke were busy with rebuilding in the city. Sir Richard, who lived mainly in London, commissioned William Cleare for his new house.[7] Cleare had connections in the capital and was perhaps linked to the Office of Works. As Wren's master joiner he made the great model for St Paul's Cathedral and designed the timber roof to span Oxford's Sheldonian Theatre in 1664, while Wren himself twice gave Sir Richard advice on technical matters in 1683.[8]

The new house was a double pile, with an 18-metre central spine wall. It had two long and impressive façades, facing 'south' and 'north', extended further by the unusual arrangement of service wings in line to each side. Thus the kitchen was, and still is, in the west pavilion, its distance originally helping to protect from fires and smells, while the granary and stables were to the east, now long removed. Both fronts were also impressive in height. The South Front had four full storeys: the ground floor for administration, the piano nobile and the floor above for the family and guests, topped by garrets in the roof for the servants. On the North Front the ground floor was half hidden by the rise of the land. Both fronts had a central flight of steps to give direct access to the piano nobile, a feature continued ever since at Stowe. In contrast, servants entered at ground-floor level on each short side from the service courts. The walls were of brick, with stone quoins, and most of the roof was tiled, apart from a balustraded lead platform for views over the garden and countryside.

The façade of each front was elegant, imitating aspects of some recent large houses in London, such as Hooke's Montagu House in Bloomsbury. Stowe's

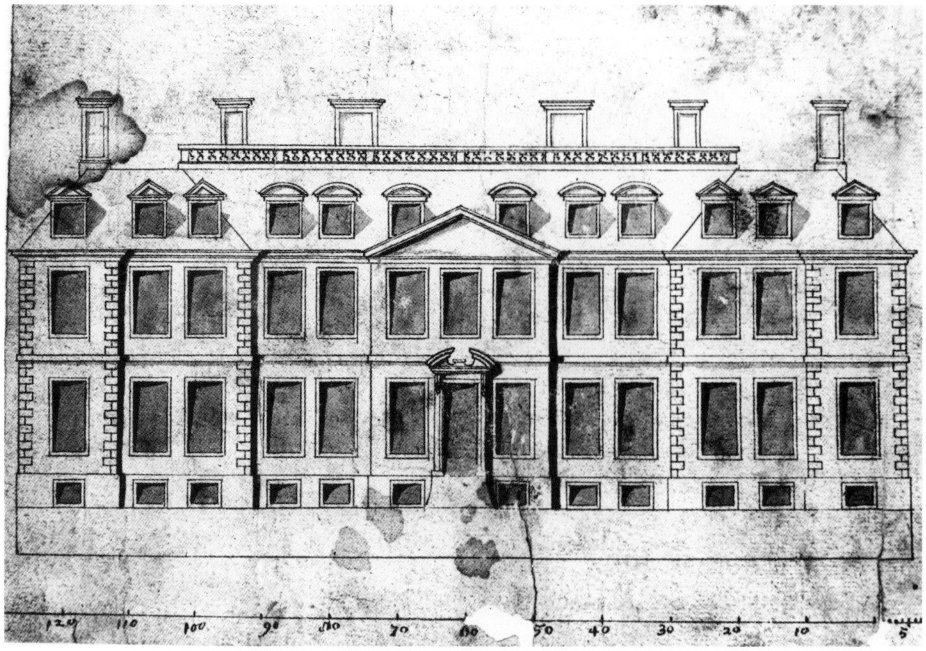

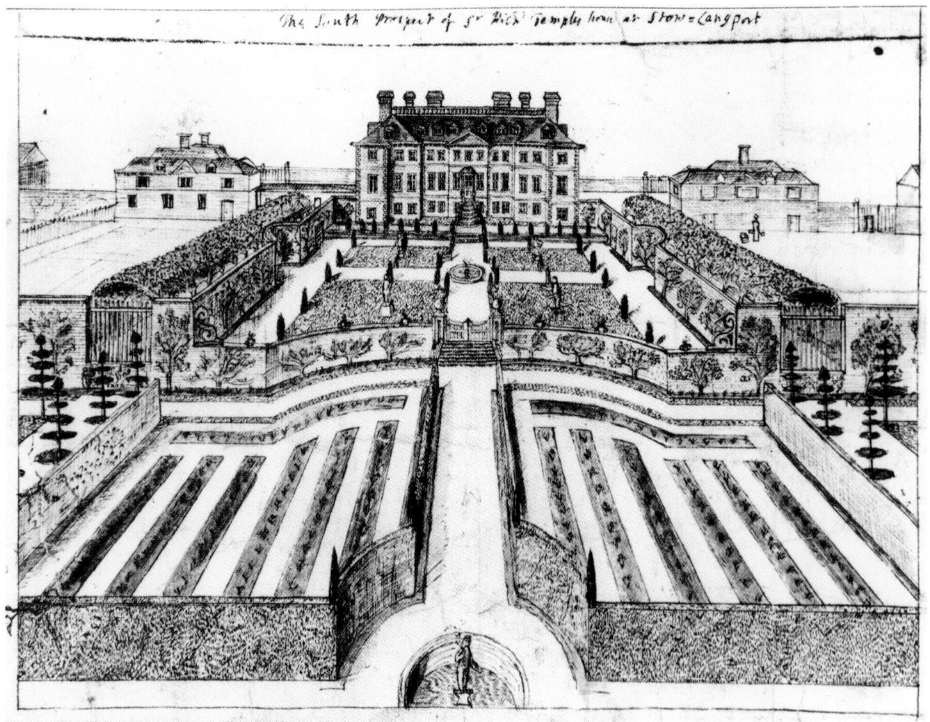

top William Cleare's design for Sir Richard Temple's house, showing the North Front, *c.*1686.

above The South Front of the house as designed by William Cleare for Sir Richard Temple, *c.*1686.

One of the North Front corner pavilions retained from the house of 1686.

central doorway in each front was emphasised by a break forwards for the central three bays, topped by a classical pediment. The new Stowe House was unusual, if not unique, in having two further breaks on each long front, giving a vigorous sense of movement and allowing the formation of distinctive corner pavilions. At two rooms deep, these corner pavilions were larger than those at Wilton, in Wiltshire, and perhaps were forerunners of Hooke's configuration at Ragley Hall, in Warwickshire. In addition, the two short sides had unusually deep recesses, creating large shadows to mask the shallow depth.

Each long front comprised of 13 bays, with perhaps six bays across the shorter ends. The house appeared imposing because of its large, numerous and closely spaced windows. The garret windows seemed crowded on the draft elevation for the North Front. These were probably rationalised, however, by the time they were constructed on the South Front. The tall chimney blocks, later removed, gave the roofline a sturdy appearance. Internally the house had 38 rooms and two cellars. The two main rooms of parade were on the piano nobile or first floor, entered by flights of steps. On the north side was a two-storey Hall, while on the south was the Great Parlour, probably slightly offset from central. To each side were secondary staircases rising the whole height of the house. To the right of the Hall, according to the draft agreement, was to be the grand staircase, but this proved difficult to fit. It was probably in a bay west of the Hall, since Celia Fiennes in about 1694 commented on the 'hall, very lofty with a gallery round the top',[9] an unlikely feature with stairs present as well.

The unusual corner pavilions, linked by wings to the central double cube at the heart of the house, enabled Sir Richard to provide suites of dressing rooms, bedrooms and closets for the use of both family and visitors. In addition, the interconnecting doorways allowed not only Fiennes's 'visto [*sic*] thro' the whole house'[10] on the north–south axis, but also enfilades running east–west. Before Fiennes's visit Sir Richard had added, perhaps in 1688, an octagonal cupola in the centre of the roof,[11] which was probably removed in the 1719 rebuilding.

left The stone-lined well underneath the south wall of the house, which was rediscovered in 2011.

Little of the original exterior is still visible, apart from, on the North Front, the two corner pavilions, perhaps parts of the original cornice and the doorway with its carved stone surround, doubtless later moved outwards to its present position. Internally the spine wall survives, along with some adjacent walls on the lower ground floor, and the brick vault north of the spine wall. In addition, sections of a secondary staircase seem to have been reused for the stairs to the north of the later west staircase. Dimensions from Cleare's plan live on, however. Thus the length of the Marble Saloon is determined by the length of Cleare's spine wall, and the centre of the Marble Saloon follows the line of Cleare's southern enfilade, a line determining the whole enfilade of State Rooms.

The stone-lined well, depicted in the sketch of about 1686 just south of the east pavilion, probably predated Cleare's plan. Its location may have helped determine the siting of Cleare's house just a short distance away from it. It was later hidden under a 1740s' wall but rediscovered in 2011. This preservation of an earlier feature is typical of Sir Richard's thrifty attitude, since he specified the reuse of material from his old house. He questioned any seemingly excessive charges, such as the cost of making bricks on the Stowe estate. Law cases and third-party adjudications ensued, while one of the two major London contractors, the bricklayer Thomas Miller, escaped to Virginia in America before the house was completed. Cleare apparently faded from the scene within a year or two, perhaps as the result of constant interference by Sir Richard and William Chaplyn, his Stowe steward. The challenge of the owners' precise architectural demands often surfaced at Stowe over the next century.

RESTRUCTURING THE CENTRAL PAVILION: LORD COBHAM, PHASE 1: VANBRUGH, KENT AND PERHAPS GIBBS, C.1719 TO THE EARLY 1730S

Sir Richard's son, another Sir Richard and later Lord Cobham, shared his father's building ambitions. He inherited in 1697, aged 21, but then served on campaign with the Duke of Marlborough. With his political and literary friends in the influential Kit-Cat Club he was well placed to take a lead in architecture, art and culture. He acquired the means in 1715 when he married Anne Halsey, with her inheritance of £20,000 from the Anchor Brewery in Southwark. First, however, in 1717 he bought out William Temple, his second cousin, from the entail of Stowe for £7,000. Cobham could now start to transform the house, helped by his share of the £87,000 prize money from his command of the Vigo campaign in 1719.

Lord Cobham initially altered Stowe House and then enlarged it. In the first phase he reconfigured the north, east and west sides, rebuilding the North Hall and probably relocating the grand staircase. Then he added two new staircases and extended the house laterally, almost tripling its size, creating an extraordinary enfilade on the piano nobile.[12]

The first phase of restructuring was masterminded by Cobham's Kit-Cat friend, Sir John Vanbrugh, the architect of Castle Howard in Yorkshire and Blenheim Palace in Oxfordshire. He visited Stowe in June 1719 and in 1725 stayed for a fortnight.[13] Probably by or in 1719, the awkward old grand staircase was removed. This allowed a new and larger North Hall to match the new Portico outside, itself similar to Vanbrugh's at Blenheim.

The North Portico, attributed to Sir John Vanbrugh.

The Orangery from the south.

The Doric arch, by Sir John Vanbrugh.

Vanbrugh also reconfigured the two service courtyards on either side of the house. He built central pavilions, rather like the Pyramid Gate at Castle Howard, at the far ends, aligned on the new North Portico. Further out to the west, he sited a brick garden building, the later Temple of Bacchus, with an Orangery to the north. On the east, he constructed a triumphal Doric archway to welcome visitors from the village road. As at Blenheim, this would have provided a dynamic view of the house to the right, marked with corner pavilions. By 1724 a tourist reported on 'Lord Cobham's at Stowe, where he has an house of 13 windows in front, with offices at both ends built by Sir John Vanbrugh.'[14] Vanbrugh probably only refaced the four long service 'offices', perhaps by Cleare, shown on an early garden plan.[15]

Apart from the North Portico, Vanbrugh also reconfigured much of the exterior of the house, according to a bird's-eye drawing. This was perhaps a sketch for the promised engraving of what had been completed by 1725,[16] or possibly a plan from 1719 of the intentions for the next six years.[17] The corner pavilions were raised as towers, the North

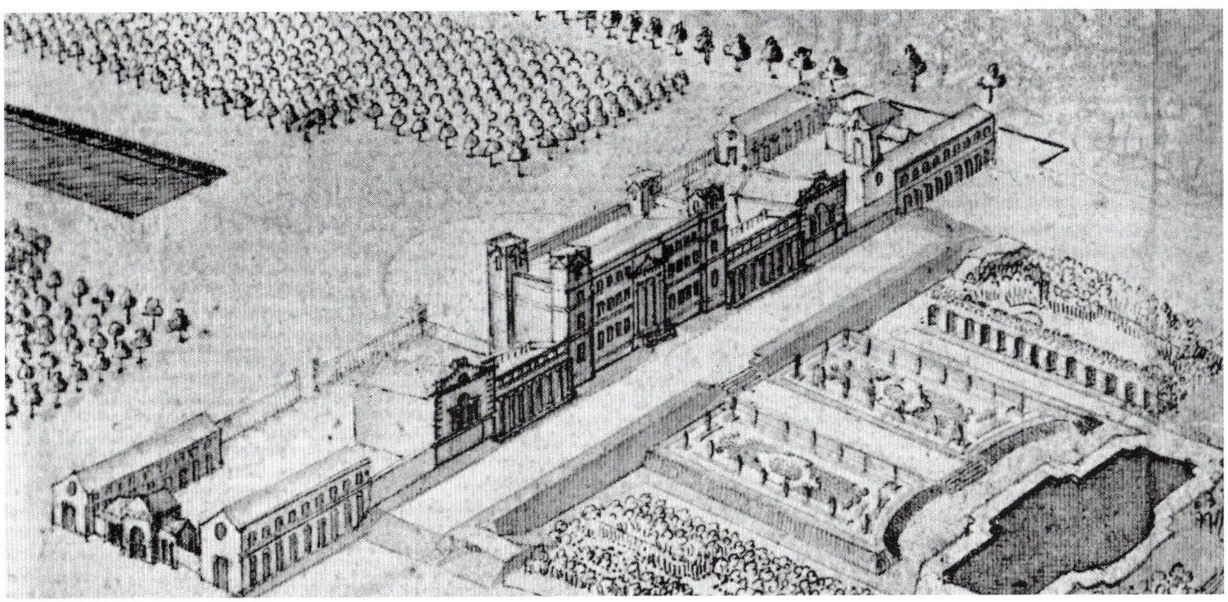

Stowe House, a detail from a bird's-eye view of the garden, by Charles Bridgeman, *c.*1719.

Front was rebuilt as a straight wall behind the Portico, and the east and west sides had their recesses filled in.

Inside, the original west secondary stairs were replaced with a delightful barrel-vault ceiling with plaster coffers. Viscount Cobham's coat of arms filled the tympanum, dating it to 1718 or after. On the east side, the old secondary stairwell was widened, probably to allow the replacement grand staircase to give access from the piano nobile to the second floor. The ceiling above had a circular space, which could have suited a painted sky, with Cobham's cipher in the corners. This then allowed the construction of the new, larger North Hall. William Kent's magnificent ceiling was a tribute to Lord Cobham as a military general. Kent's plan for the room shows suggestions by perhaps Henry Flitcroft, who was working with Kent at nearby Ditchley in 1726.[18] In 2016 a *trompe-l'oeil* painting was discovered on the north wall of the eastern landing. Showing Minerva, the classical goddess of war, standing in a niche (see p. 118), it matches the martial theme of Kent's ceiling in the North Hall, the 'Fame and Victory' painting over the east staircase (see p. 115), and the set of 'Art of War' tapestries hung in the Great Parlour by 1711 to commemorate Cobham's part in Marlborough's campaign.[19]

In 1731 a visitor reported that 'the Rooms above Stairs were beautifying, so that we lost sight of the Pictures there', but by 1735 Christophe Veyrier's relief in the North Hall and a two-tier South Portico had been added, to 'very good effect', along with the 'four blunt Turrets, one at each corner, which is also a late addition', which John Loveday did not like.[20] The house remained bare brick.[21] Kent, or possibly James Gibbs who was at Stowe from 1726, may have added these features. Kent also built two large gateways on the northern side of each service courtyard.

Cobham built the New Inn in 1717, turning Stowe into a visitor attraction. His first phase of remodelling under Vanbrugh and others succeeded in producing a more fashionable house. By the 1730s Stowe had become a literary centre and was attracting many visitors.[22] From 1731 poems, engravings and descriptions of the house and garden were published to feed the growing market. Yet increasingly the mansion seemed too small. Cobham was a leading politician whose 'cubs' led opposition to Robert Walpole, the Prime Minister. When Walpole deprived Cobham of his regiment after Cobham voted against Walpole's controversial Excise Bill in 1733, Cobham retired to Stowe to make yet further extensions to his house and garden.

opposite above The North Hall ceiling central panel.

opposite below William Kent's gateway, built into the screen walls in about 1780.

ENLARGING THE HOUSE: LORD COBHAM, PHASE 2: GIBBS AND BROWN, THE LATE 1730S TO 1749

The motivation to expand his house was probably partly dynastic. Cobham's marriage of 1715 remained childless, so in 1736 he agreed to settle Stowe at his death on Richard Grenville, his eldest nephew. This enabled Grenville, or Earl Temple as he was to become after his uncle's death in 1749 and his mother's in 1752, to marry Anna Chamber in 1737. She had inherited £50,000 from her father – her grandfather had been the East India Company agent in Madras – making Grenville, 'perhaps the ablest financier in Europe',[23] allegedly the richest commoner in the kingdom.

New staircases

Cobham's challenge was to add space to his reconfigured house. One problem was the Great Parlour, which would eventually have to be enlarged to balance the new North Hall. The result of taking out the gallery in the old Hall, as well as the grand staircase from the west side, and replacing the western service stairs with the coffered barrel vault, was that the second floor on the west had been almost cut off. The only remaining access would have been through the interconnecting rooms above. These, however, would also be removed when the Great Parlour was extended vertically. Therefore, a new grand staircase was needed on the west side. But to keep the coffered vault would require a bay built further out. Moreover, to maintain symmetry, it would be necessary to have a matching staircase extension on the east side. These two stairwells, facing each other with their fine cantilevered stairs, date from between 1733 (Jacques Rigaud's drawings) and 1750 (George Bickham's and Benton Seeley's engravings).

There was no urgency to rebuild the south side of the central pavilion itself with its new double-tier South Portico. In fact, this Portico and the Great Parlour were not rebuilt for almost 40 years, since the grand enfilade, with its suite of interconnected State Rooms, could still take shape independently.

New stables

Before further rooms could be added to the east pavilion, the old stables doubtless had to be removed. These were rebuilt on the north-east corner of the service court, echoing the location of Vanbrugh's Orangery on the north-west. The central three bays of the new stables imitated Vanbrugh's courtyard pavilion, with a high central arch capped by a pediment.

East pavilion and Ballroom: 'Grenville' rooms

The lateral expansion began on the east side, continuing from the east staircase bay. In 1742 his Lordship was apparently 'annually adding to and improving' the house.[24] The five new rooms on the

The west staircase.

The coffered barrel-vault ceiling in the West Corridor.

far left The south front of Grafton House, built as stables *c.*1742, adapted in 1926 by Clough Williams-Ellis and now boarding accommodation.

left Part of the enlarged house: the east pavilion today.

east consisted of a Ballroom (now the Library), Drawing Room (Blue Room), Dressing Room and Bedchamber (Chandos House dormitories), and a Chapel (Aurelian Room) to the north.

The Ballroom used the south wall of the eastern stairwell as part of its north wall. It was mainly all new, raised above and in front of the old passageway, but keeping the pattern of seven bays shown in Rigaud's 1733 drawing.

The family Chapel was located behind the east end of the Ballroom, across the piano nobile passage. It thus looked over the east courtyard. Although the main body of the Chapel was on the ground floor, suiting use by the servants, its balcony for the family was at the level of the piano nobile. Its ceiling was copied from the Chapel Royal at St James's Palace, itself taken from an engraving by Sebastiano Serlio.[25]

The Chapel and nearby Drawing Room became 'Grenville' rooms, in recognition of Stowe's designated heir. By 1746–47 the Chapel featured cedar panelling, now mostly in Sir Robert Lorimer's School Chapel, previously removed from Stowe House in Cornwall, another Grenville house, after its demolition in 1739. Similarly, the Drawing Room was called in 1748 the 'Grenville' room, 'hung with whole lengths of all the Grenville family.'[26] The Dressing Room and Bedchamber completing the eastern end of the enfilade were described as those of Lady Cobham, with Chinese and Indian decorations.

West pavilion and State Apartments

At the opposite end of the house Cobham planned the State Apartments, with the State Bedchamber at the west end mirroring Lady Cobham's Bedchamber at the east end. The State Gallery (the State Dining Room) provided access, mirroring the Ballroom

above A view of the house from the parterre, by Jacques Rigaud, published in 1739.

left The gallery of the former Chapel, photographed by J. Mudd in the 1870s.

opposite The ceiling of the former Chapel (now the Aurelian Room).

HOUSEMASTER

(the Library). The Gallery had joiners and carpenters at work in 1746 with painting continuing to 1750.

The romantic and artistic sensibility of Earl Temple's wife, Anna Grenville, can perhaps be seen in the first two of these three rooms. The Gallery's dominant feature were the five fine Brussels tapestries of 'Triumphs of the Gods', commissioned in 1747 from Daniel Leyniers specially for this room.[27] Their arrangement focused on love, with the vast 'Triumph of Venus' holding centre stage on the long wall. At the ends were two other central tapestries, also of females, Ceres and Diana, leaving the pair of male gods, Bacchus and Mars, for the corners. To emphasise the theme of love, the three central ceiling flats probably held, as now, scenes of Venus. Likewise in the cove, two of the four roundels were of Cupid, along with some playful naturalistic animal scenes. Moreover, the subject matter of the wooden reliefs in the chimney overmantels, 'A Goddess conducting Learning to Truth' and 'Mercury conducting Tragedy and Comedy to Parnassus', fits well with Anna's poetic and dramatic compositions.

Anna Grenville may also have been involved in the unusual overmantel for the adjoining room, described as a Drawing Room by Lady Newdigate in 1748. It held a portrait of Lord Cobham by Sir Godfrey Kneller. This could be seen as a tribute to their uncle by the future owners, fitting with his coats of arms on the Brussels tapestries in the adjoining Gallery, and linked with his arms on the 'Art of War' tapestries later hung in this room.

The final western room was 'a prodigious large bedchamber', still just brick walls in 1748, reputedly costing £10,000.[28] From the start it was designed to hold the State Bed on a raised dais, but it was not fitted up until Earl Temple's time.

Architects: James Gibbs and Lancelot Brown

Some clues exist for the architects of Cobham's second phase of building. James Gibbs is probably

Decorative detailing in the Blue Room.

the key person. In 1748 Lady Newdigate commented that 'There are two Noble Apartments newly built, a Ball room … a drawing room'. These two rooms, or the Chapel, may be those mentioned in the summary of Gibbs's work for Cobham at Stowe: 'likewise additions to his countray house there, wher there are two noble apartments finely finished, besides others for strangers'.[29] Details like the bold entablature and cornice in the Blue Room, where James Lovell later, in 1774–75, added to the ceiling only four plaster reliefs, the Greek guilloche above the cornice in the Library and the ceiling cherubs in the Chapel, are all typical of Gibbs. The external window surrounds on the stairwells added to the central pavilion are also representative of his work. This suggests that Gibbs, along with Cobham, proposed the far-sighted scheme of enlarging the house along the piano nobile using the south enfilade in the existing central pavilion as the northern enfilade of the new line of reception rooms.

The Stable Block may also be by Gibbs, who might have been involved in redesigning the house at an earlier stage, from 1726 after Vanbrugh's death. In this case Vanbrugh might have relocated the grand staircase in 1719, added the North Portico and started to create the North Hall, leaving Gibbs to complete the North Hall, east and west house walls and new fronts for the link corridors and pavilions, as shown in Rigaud's 1733 drawings. Then Kent may have arrived from about 1728 to add the interior decorations for the North Hall, Grenville Landing and coffered vault passage, later building his gateways, capping the towers and providing the double South Portico.

Lancelot 'Capability' Brown was also involved as an architect, since he was asked for his plan for the 'Long Room' in 1747, when work was taking place in both the Long Room and the Great Room, possibly the Ballroom (now the Library) and the Gallery (now the State Dining Room) respectively.[30] He learnt his skills as an architect at Stowe, copying Gibbs. In fact, he may have been responsible for a large amount of the basic building work during the 1740s, since much of it was simply an adaptation of existing buildings planned probably by Gibbs, which a builder or clerk of works like Brown could easily copy. This may explain the uneven appearance of the South Front by 1750 and the absence of an architect's name. Even the new stables were little more than a copy of Vanbrugh's end pavilion with low functional wings attached on each side. Like other architects working on the house, Brown added garden buildings, as well as the Grecian Temple,[31] Lord Cobham's pillar and perhaps the Lady's Temple.

Another architectural contender is Fli(n)tcroft. He was given 6 guineas as a present in 1737. This is small

A detail of the house in Jacques Rigaud's view from the parterre, published in 1739 (see also p. 40).

The State Dining Room, 1921, showing Daniel Leyniers's tapestries.

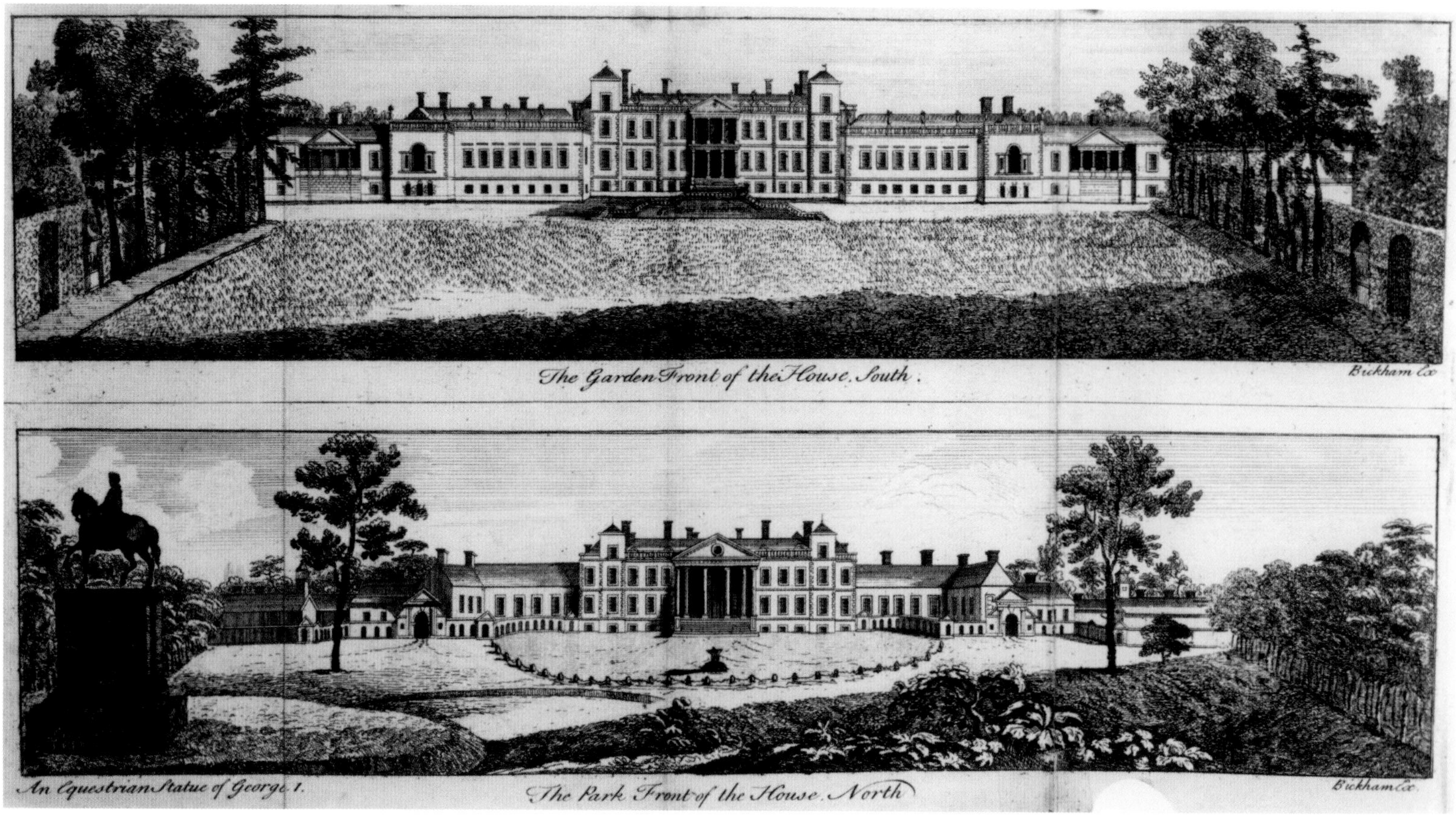

The South and North Fronts of Stowe House, by George Bickham, as published by Benton Seeley in 1750.

for major rebuilding works, however, and more likely refers either to the Chinese House or possibly to the west corridor vault.[32]

Lord Cobham's architectural achievement

In 1748, the year before Cobham's death, Stowe was described as the longest house in England, with an enfilade of over 137 metres within a front stretching for more than 274 metres. Externally it was impressive: 'being Whited Over has a very good Effect'.[33] Another visitor described it as 'presque toute neuve' and 'tout y est dans le goût modern'.[34] By 1750 George Bickham claimed that Stowe had 'some of the finest Rooms perhaps in Europe'.[35]

NEOCLASSICAL GRANDEUR: EARL TEMPLE, 1749 TO 1779

Earl Temple inherited Stowe in 1749. From the start he was an enthusiast for the latest archaeological evidence of classical precedents. Cobham's eclectic approach had allowed Vanbrugh's Hellenistic Rotunda and Egyptian Pyramid, a Palladian Bridge, Gibbs's Gothic Temple of Liberty, Brown's Grecian Temple and a Roman rostral column. In contrast, Temple wanted neoclassical accuracy, seeking to replicate authentic classical exemplars. Thus the State Bedchamber imitated a temple from Palmyra, the South Portico featured the Lysicrates Monument and the Marble Saloon was a stunning evocation of the greatest of classical interiors, that of the Pantheon in Rome.

Secondly, Temple wished to adorn Stowe with real classical antiquities. Thus, in 1774 he sent his nephew and heir to collect antique statues from Italy to populate the niches in his Marble Saloon and South Portico.

Thirdly, Temple wanted architects with classical expertise. In about 1752 he commissioned Giovanni Battista Borra to design the State Bedchamber and redesign the South Front. Borra was the draftsman who had accompanied Robert Wood and James Dawkins to Palmyra and Baalbcc in 1751. This was the first systematic archaeological expedition and it helped to inspire the neoclassical.[36] Georges-François Blondel, who had spent some time in Rome, also produced a plan for the South Front.[37] Having studied at Parma and Rome, Vincenzo Valdrè became Temple's decorator of choice, working in the Marble Saloon, the State Drawing Room and the State Music Room.

Fourthly, Temple, like other members of his family, through numerous contacts became highly

Giovanni Battista Borra's 1752 scheme for the South Front of Stowe (unrealised).

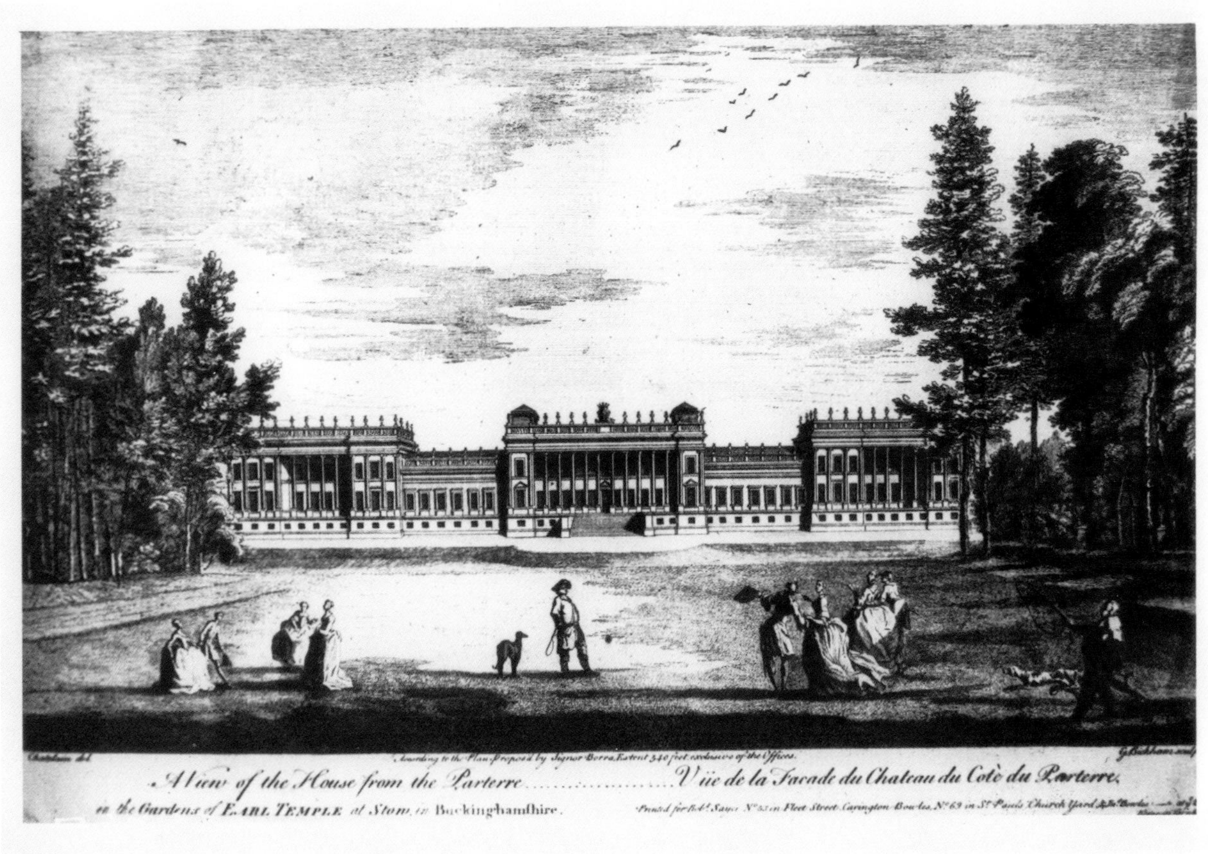

knowledgeable about classical architecture. Thus he designed with Borra a new flight of steps for the South Front in 1754 and could challenge experts like Robert Adam over incorrect use of vertical fluting in the frieze of an Ionic entablature. He shared this architectural enthusiasm with his brother-in-law, William Pitt, and his cousin, Thomas Pitt.[38]

The State Bedchamber: the first authentic neoclassical interior

Earl Temple's initial challenge was to finish the interiors of the three State Apartments at the west end. The Gallery was still being painted in 1750 while in 1755 Borra designed the overmantel for the State Dressing Room next door.

The State Bedchamber was the finale of the grand enfilade, Temple's axis of honour. It can claim to be by far the most important architectural addition to Stowe House. Although the later Marble Saloon is more spectacular and the State Music Room more exquisitely charming, the original State Bedchamber was probably the first serious attempt at a neoclassical interior based on authentic records of an extant building.[39] However, just as its prototype in Palmyra, Syria, was destroyed in August 2015,[40] so most of the original interior at Stowe was removed in 1936 because of dry rot. The Palmyrene corner closets, with their Corinthian half-columns, were not replaced and the replica Palmyrene ceiling is no longer centred on the enfilade.

The interior of the State Bedchamber was designed from 1752 by Borra after his arrival in London to prepare his drawings for the *Ruins of Palmyra* published in 1753.[41] The room was constructed by John Hobcraft from 1755. The unique floor plan matched the four corner closets of the Temple of Palmyra, while the main ceiling imitated the most iconic of the four types of Palmyrene ceilings, composed of regular octagons joined at the angles. The loggia later had two of the other three Palmyrene ceiling types.

Although Borra's State Bed, erected in 1759 and forming the focal point for the enfilade, boasted imperial fasces on its columns, this Palmyrene room could fit with the feminine feel of the Gallery. Palmyra's Zenobia, the 'noblest woman in all the orient', was a model for a successful leader of a republican trading and military state, whose minister Longinus was the author of the treatise *On the Sublime* (first century AD). The room was also to become a tribute to Earl Temple himself: a Temple interior as

The Garter Room, *c.*1926, in use as a dining room.

Detail from R. Wood, *The Ruins of Palmyra* (1753).

Decorative details inspired by Palmyra on the ceiling of the former State Bedchamber.

the climax of the grand enfilade in Temple's house. He had to wait until 1760, however, to add the Garter insignia to the ceiling, positioned like a radiant sun in the centre. His brother-in-law, the elder Pitt, had asked King George II for it in 1759, but the king's hostility to Temple's ambition delayed its grant by a year.

Preparing for rebuilding the two fronts

Completing the interiors of the three State Rooms was straightforward compared with reconfiguring the southern centre of the house. Ever since the 1730s–40s, when the stairwells were added to each side of the central pavilion, the plan must have been to rebuild the offset Great Parlour into a grand double-height reception saloon. This would involve reconstructing the entire South Front into a unified neoclassical palace.[42]

Earl Temple commissioned a scheme from Borra in 1752, but William Pitt exposed its weaknesses and it was never executed. A plan engraved in 1763 shows another unbuilt scheme, apart from some external stairs, designed by Temple and Borra in 1754. In 1766, to provide additional rooms when much of the centre of the house would be unusable because of the rebuilding, Temple subdivided the Ballroom into a Drawing Room and a Dining Room. He also commissioned another scheme, from Blondel, but again this was not executed. Nevertheless, Blondel's plan for the area that is now the Marble Saloon may have suggested the role of classical sculpture.

As well as a plan, Temple needed money. This came in part from his nephew and successor, George Grenville. From the age of 11, thanks to his father the Prime Minister, George had received the sinecure income of a Teller of the Exchequer. In 1770 George offered this, about £3,000 annually, towards rebuilding the South Front.[43] The Marble Saloon alone was said to have cost £12,000.

The insignia of the Order of the Garter on the ceiling of the former State Bedchamber (now the Garter Room).

The North Front

Temple started with the North Front. There were several alterations to the plan, as advised by William Pitt and Thomas Pitt, who formed his informal 'committee of taste'.[44] It was built rapidly, with changes made to the roof of the east colonnade while building was underway. Attic walls were later added to the garret floor, while the screen walls, enlivened by herms,[45] were raised to hide the service courtyards, and the Kent gateways were moved further out to improve the appearance.

The South Front

Temple took even longer to decide on the South Front.[46] Blondel's plan was impressive but too fussy. A second plan by Robert and James Adam was close to what was built, but Thomas Pitt wisely reduced the three different sizes of classical orders to two, giving both harmony and splendour. The slight flatness of the design was enlivened by the projecting South Portico and the grand sweep of steps down into the garden, Temple's own idea and improving on Adam's vertical wall. A start was made in 1771 but even then the foundations were dug up soon afterwards. By 1776 Lord Nuneham described it as surpassing 'in majesty and beauty everything I have seen'.[47] More recently it has been called 'a composition which is hard to match in England for monumental dignity and classical poise'.[48]

Sculpture

Classical sculpture was a key element of Temple's scheme. He sent his nephew on a Grand Tour in 1774 to collect statues for the South Portico and the Marble Saloon.[49] He commissioned a new relief sculpture for the North Hall,[50] as a pendant to Veyrier's relief bought by his uncle.[51] He added the pair of Coade lions

The figure of Liberty on the South Front is distinguished by its squint.

The Lysicrates frieze in the South Portico, which is believed to portray Earl Temple feeding a lion representing Britain.

A Coade stone lion on the North Front.

to the North Portico in 1778.[52] At one stage Temple planned a triumphal statue of King William III on the apex of the South Portico, extolling the Glorious Revolution. Lovell carved eight medallions and four skyline figures in Portland stone based on classical themes, while new and antique statues enlivened the Portico.[53]

The South Portico also boasted a version of the frieze from the Lysicrates Monument in Athens, taken from James Stuart and Nicholas Revett's 1762 publication.[54] In the centre a lanky Bacchus feeds a lion, perhaps hinting at 'long-legged' Temple's support for Britain, the lion. George Clarke has likewise explained how atop the west pavilion, 18 metres from the ground and therefore impossible to see with the naked eye, the classical figure of Liberty was made with a squint, a clear reference to the libertarian politician John Wilkes, from Aylesbury. Temple had secretly supported him in his claim to individual rights against the oppressive actions of the then government, led by Temple's own brother, George Grenville.[55]

Marble Saloon

One of Temple's greatest achievements in rebuilding the South Front was to create the three superb rooms in the central pavilion. At their heart was the stunning Marble Saloon: the focal point of both the north–south axis and the line of the enfilade. It was modelled on the Pantheon in Rome but more dramatic with its elliptical rather than circular plan. Valdrè skilfully designed the coffering in ever-smaller bands around the central oculus, while the unique triumphal frieze, inspired by the Parthenon and by Roman reliefs, likewise uses foreshortening. The double-height doorways emphasise the vertical axis, while the plain floor and unusually shallow niches enliven the horizontal dynamic. The plasterwork took William Peart longer than anticipated and the Saloon was eventually completed under the Marquess of Buckingham, Temple's nephew and successor.

The Marble Saloon frieze, showing a detail of the triumphal procession.

The Marble Saloon, with its coffered ceiling, houses classical statues in the niches around its circumference.

At the top of the dome of the Marble Saloon are the arms of the Marquess of Buckingham (*left above*), under whom the work was completed, and Earl Temple (*left below*), who commissioned it.

below An Athénienne in the Marble Saloon.

bottom An engraving of the Marble Saloon, artist unknown, 1783–88.

The State Music Room

George Grenville, subsequently the Marquess of Buckingham, inherited Stowe in 1779. He first finished his uncle's interiors.[56] The Marble Saloon has both his and his uncle's coats of arms either side of the oculus. To the east lies the State Music Room, Valdrè's exquisite masterpiece,[57] with its copies of Raphael's classical wall paintings, inspired by ancient 'grotesque' decorations discovered in Rome. In the centre of its west wall he depicted an open temple for Apollo, god of music, with a tribute to Lady Buckingham, both a musician and artist. Valdrè's circular painting in the centre of the ceiling reflects Apollo's role as sun god, with dawn, night, the hours and the seasons travelling lightly around the radiating boss and central chandelier.

The central ceiling painting in the State Music Room: *Dance of the Hours*, by Vincenzo Valdrè, 1788.

left The State Music Room restored to its former glory.

above A panel featuring Apollo in the State Music Room.

The State Drawing Room

The Marquess also completed the State Drawing Room, the companion room lying to the west of the Marble Saloon. Here he showed his antiquarian interests by having a chimney piece that included an ancient relief sculpture,[58] while the columns were carved wood with paint and gilding, below an unusual entablature with its curved frieze. The ceiling is restrained, with plaster relief and other classical motifs. This focused visual attention on the walls with their crimson damask and the best of the picture collection.

above A watercolour by Joseph Nash showing a lady in black, perhaps meant to represent Queen Victoria, in the State Drawing Room, 1845.

right The State Drawing Room, *c.*1870, now known as the Temple Room, having served as the Common Room for the boarding house of that name.

The South Front balustrade.

The South Front balustrade

In 1781 the future Marquess commissioned from John Cheere a pair of 'Medici' lions to guard the foot of the steps, using Matthew Brettingham's mould.[59] As the number of visitors to the house increased, in 1790 the Marquess added the balustrade along the South Front to keep people away from the private apartments on the ground floor. Earlier, in 1780, a delightful Ménagerie had been built for Lady Buckingham as a place where she could find some peace, although it later became part of the visitor route in its own right. In 1805 the Marquess also reduced the height of the walls flanking the steps.

The Egyptian Hall

The Marquess inherited the family passion for architecture and in 1803, inspired by discoveries from Napoleon Bonaparte's expedition to Egypt, designed the Egyptian Hall as a winter entrance below the North Hall, adjoining a new porte cochère. The sloping walls with canvas paintings were copied from engravings, while the classical sarcophagus hid a heating system, a concept with which Sir John Soane experimented in several other houses.[60]

The Egyptian Hall with representations of classical paintings and a replica sarcophagus.

Furnished for twenty-first-century educational needs, the Library retains its eighteenth-century mahogany bookcases installed by the book-loving Marquess and has been enhanced by the addition of replicas of the unique lanterns.

The Library and the Gothic Library

The Marquess's main interest, however, was books and manuscripts. In 1792, therefore, he reunified the old Ballroom, which had been temporarily split into two, as the large Library, to house some 20,000 books. As his collection expanded he added a gallery and then turned the adjoining room into a library too. He also employed Soane in 1805 to design his Saxon Room, now the Gothic Library, for his Saxon and Irish manuscripts.[61] Although Soane had worked for the Marquess in the classical style on his Pall Mall house in 1790–94,[62] this was Soane's only Gothic interior, a result of the Marquess's dynastic interest. His son's marriage in 1796 to Anna Eliza Brydges made his grandson, the later 2nd Duke, a direct Plantagenet descendant in the twelfth generation from King Henry VII. He therefore set a relief of the battle of Bosworth over the doorway and insisted that the room imitated elements of King Henry VII's Chapel in Westminster Abbey.

opposite Sir John Soane's Gothic Library, built to house Saxon manuscripts, now serves as the Headmaster's Study.

above The Bosworth relief over the door to the Gothic Library.

right The delicate tracery over the fireplace in the Gothic Library is modelled on that of Henry VII's Chapel in Westminster Abbey.

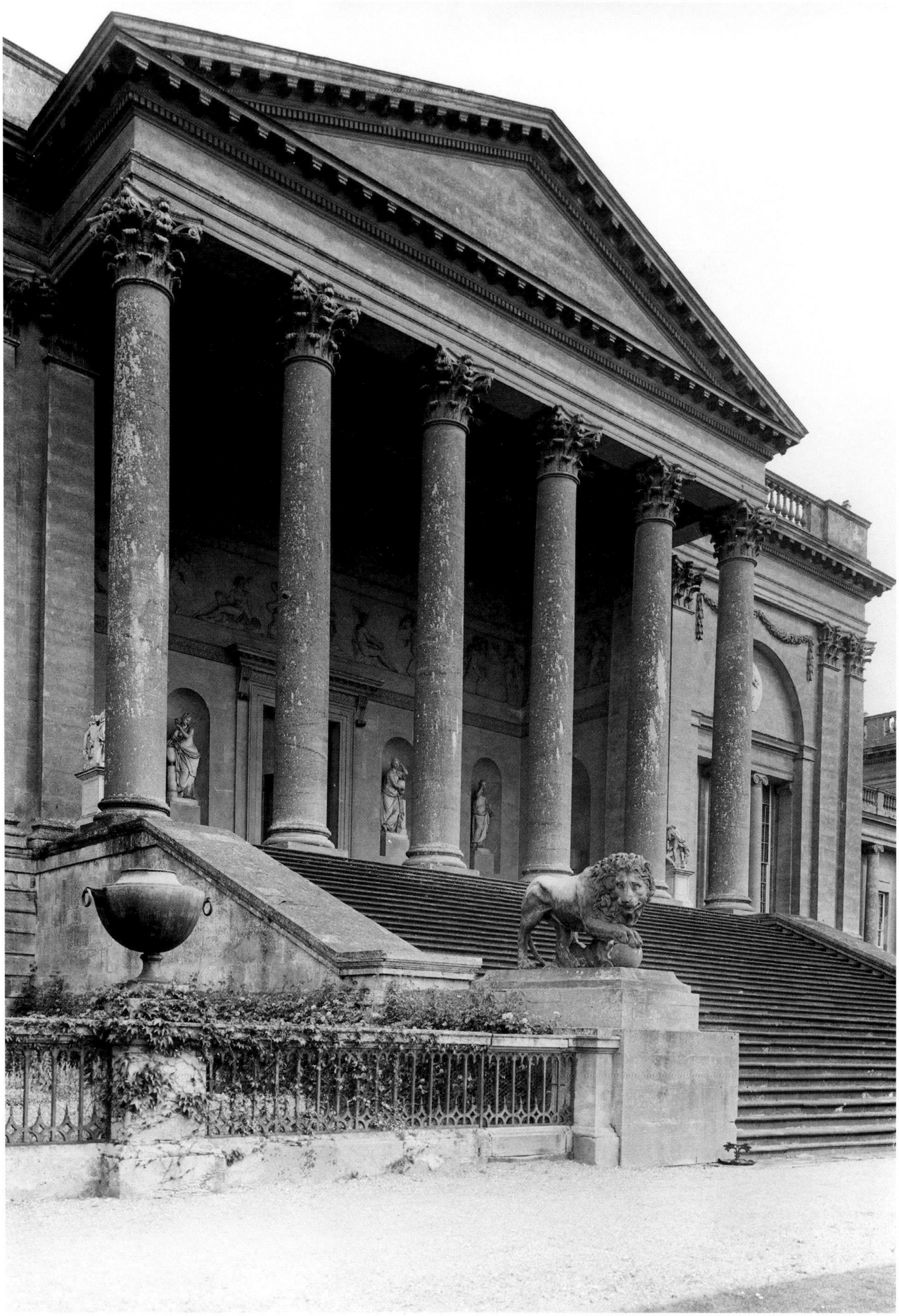

The South Front in 1914.

FADING GLORY: THE DUKES OF BUCKINGHAM AND CHANDOS, AND LADY KINLOSS, 1813–1922

The 1st Duke had grand schemes but little money. In 1817–18 Soane and Lady Grenville planned to turn the service wing at the west end of the house, now Nugent House, into a new suite of reception rooms overlooking the Orangery Garden, but these were not executed.[63] The 2nd Duke, even more in debt, closed the house to visitors and employed Edward Blore for minor refurbishment, including the addition of some water closets, prior to the visit by Queen Victoria in 1845.[64] Elizabeth George from nearby Dadford complained about the costly changes made before the royal visit, which 'so crowded the apartments as to give them the appearance of a large furniture warehouse'. Preparations for the royal visit merely added to the Duke's debts, leading to the great sale of the contents by Christie's for 40 days in 1848.[65]

The 3rd Duke moved back to Stowe from the old Grenville seat in Wotton Underwood, Buckinghamshire, in 1862. He refurbished the Blue Room and installed a gasworks and lighting.[66] When he died in 1889 the house was let to the Comte de Paris, the pretender to the French throne.[67] In 1921 the family sold the house and remaining contents.[68] The purchaser, Harry Shaw, apparently failed to complete, so Stowe House was sold again in 1922, when it was saved from demolition by being bought for Stowe School.

The portrait of J.F. Roxburgh, Stowe School's first Headmaster, surveys the elegant Ante-Library.

PERSTO ET PRÆSTO
INGREDIENTES EXEVNTESQVE CVSTODI DOMINE DEVS

opposite Sir Robert Lorimer's Chapel with, in the foreground, a bust of Old Stoic humanitarian Leonard Cheshire (Lord Cheshire of Woodhall).

below Afternoon sunshine on the South Front of Stowe House, still a distinguished seat of learning over 200 years after its completion.

following pages Stowe House and the landscape garden are indivisible: the view from the South Portico.

REJUVENATION: STOWE SCHOOL, 1922–1997

When Stowe House was put up for sale, Clough Williams-Ellis could see its importance and possibilities.[69] He was appointed as the first architect to Stowe School and John Fergusson Roxburgh (known as JF) became the first Headmaster. He quickly established Stowe as a leading public school from 1923.[70] Williams-Ellis converted the bedrooms and service quarters into boarding houses, and installed necessary services. He added accommodation blocks in the two service courtyards. At first lessons were held in the State Rooms but soon the main house provided accommodation, dining halls and the Headmaster's study.[71] The new Chapel of 1927, designed by Sir Robert Lorimer,[72] was sited west of the house, like most of the School's new buildings,[73] such as the Art School and some buildings by R. Fielding Dodd in the 1930s.[74]

The School began repairs to the South Front, North Front and Garter Room in the 1930s and, in the 1960s, adopted a programme of restoration to the main State Rooms, using restorers such as Michael and Benjamin Gibbon. Since 1989 there have been further external repairs and systems installed for fire protection and detection. The School opened the house and garden to visitors in 1974, with displays and a circuit tour from 1990. The SHPT was established in 1997 and, in 1999, the School Governors granted it a 99-year lease on the house to permit restoration and public access.[75] A Welcome Centre was added on the ground floor in 2005 and enlarged in 2015. This Centre tells the story of Stowe House, from the creative influences that inspired its design through the extravagance that brought about its decline, to its rescue by Stowe School and its restoration under the SHPT. Once again, a house that led the way in opening its doors to visitors in the eighteenth century has shown innovation in visitor management and historical interpretation.

Chapter Three

Restoring Magnificence: The Work of the Stowe House Preservation Trust

NICK MORRIS

One of the beautifully restored decorated panels in the State Music Room.

Many aspects of the restoration of Stowe are impressive; if nothing else, the cost and the scale are of staggering proportions, while the challenges faced in delivering the work with minimal disruption to the daily life of a leading independent school are significant and, of course, the results almost defy superlatives. To see the South Front radiating warmth on a summer's day or to absorb the sumptuous feel of the Blue Room, the grandeur of the State Music Room or the understated classicism of the Library are all experiences that leave a lasting impression. Above all that, however, the breadth of skills and the professionalism of those involved during the past 18 years in delivering these projects stand as testimony to a level of expertise that would have satisfied even the most demanding of Stowe's previous owners. This chapter includes the accounts of a number of experts who have honoured the Stowe House Preservation Trust (SHPT) with their services and expertise. We start with Jane Kennedy, a partner in Purcell Architects (formerly Purcell Miller Tritton), who gives her record of the conservation and restoration of the exteriors and interiors of the house. The architect's task begins a long time ahead of the actual project, with the convening of a design team to assess the accumulated research, agree the decorative scheme and materials and then to bring together the whole project plan. It is the architect who leads much of this process, while the client (in this case the SHPT) secures the funding, calculates the time available for the work and considers the risks that might occur along the way.

At Stowe, we have placed much emphasis on the importance of scholarly research; put simply, we do not do anything to the house without firm evidence that we are restoring it to a condition in which it appeared at the appropriate time in its history. We are fortunate that a substantial part of our archive has survived and is housed in the Huntington Library in San Marino, California. Bought by Henry E. Huntington to add to his collections of works of art and other archives, it is held in a library available for scholars to appreciate and examine for a wide variety of academic purposes. The disadvantage of distance from Stowe is compensated by the marvellous surroundings and the fact that the archive remains intact, while we are privileged to have a good relationship with staff at the Huntington and to have the service of a local architect, Cathy Fisher, who conducts painstaking research on our behalf. The building at Stowe also tells us an enormous amount: physical research can sometimes start only once work has begun and floors, walls and ceilings have been opened up.

All restoration projects at Stowe draw heavily on the archives housed in the Huntington Library, California, but their exploitation requires a painstaking review of bundles of papers.

Where possible, all such research is undertaken in advance of the restoration to enable planning and budgeting and it is supplemented by physical investigations of the building fabric. One such example is the analysis of previous paint schemes. Patrick Baty, who has analysed historical paint schemes worldwide, outlines his experience in this field in the second of the following essays, demonstrating the alliance of high technology and historical understanding to show how we arrive at the paint schemes for walls, ceilings and woodwork at Stowe. Archival research demands meticulous attention to detail and persistence as explained by Annabel Westman, an expert in historic textiles and fabrics whose advice was invaluable when we set out to trace the pattern for the silk damask in the magnificent Blue Room. Annabel's essay explains how, starting with black and white photographs and descriptions, an appropriate pattern and the finishing details were achieved.

Photographs usually provide a reliable source of evidence but contemporary prints may give a distorted representation of how a room or a finishing detail appeared at the time they were sketched. This was the case with images of the Egyptian Hall, of which only two were available. Here we allowed ourselves some latitude in interpreting the images shown in the sketches of the wall paintings. John Maddison won a commission to reproduce as closely as possible the wall paintings, while also giving them an unmistakably contemporary look and he explains how this was done, to spectacular effect. In the Library and State Music Room, different challenges were faced when trying to agree designs for lighting. For the State Music Room, we were fortunate to have photographs of the exact chandelier before it was sold in 1920 but the only evidence available for the Library was two eighteenth-century sketches, one in black and white. John Darlington, who secured donations for replica lights for both rooms, explains the process from sketching to mock-ups that finally allowed the manufacture of copies that match the originals as closely as possible.

Visitors will notice that Stowe has few items of furniture or artefacts on display and Anna McEvoy,

Monitoring the progress of stonework repairs.

Vincenzo Valdrè's *Dance of the Hours*: restoration in progress showing the removal of overpainting (*above left*), the condition of the work before restoration (*above right*) and a detail (*below*) showing, on the left-hand side, the work before cleaning, and on the right-hand side, after.

Restoring the ceiling in the North Hall.

Stonemasons at work on the South Front and the finished work radiating warmth from the sunshine.

the house custodian, outlines the reasons for this, while providing a tantalising glimpse into the glories that the house once contained and explaining the campaign to trace fixtures and fittings as part of our quest to expand our knowledge of the mansion as it was in its heyday. Sometimes, we have been fortunate enough to recover items of significance, such as Vincenzo Valdrè's great painting, *Dance of the Hours*, based on Guido Reni's masterpiece that was much vaunted in the houses of those who had completed the Grand Tour. Also of Grand Tour provenance are Stowe's Medici lions, which were returned to their majestic positions on the South Front thanks to the generosity of Blackpool Corporation and the professional attention of Rupert Harris who describes his work in conserving the originals and creating exact replicas for continued display in Blackpool. The innovative arrangements agreed with Blackpool Corporation have established a link with the town that is maintained by Stowe School's musicians performing at a number of events there every summer. We are also fortunate to have copies of the statues that once adorned the South Portico, whose owners gave permission for reproductions to be made so that visitors to Stowe could better appreciate the presentation of the house as it was in the eighteenth century. Trevor Proudfoot, of Cliveden Conservation, describes the process of manufacturing and restoring stone statuary for this stage in the restoration process. Fittingly, as this book is being published in 2018, the year that marks the tercentenary of Cobham's elevation to the Viscountcy, his essay also recounts work to restore the figure of Cobham, who surveys his estate from atop the lofty pillar to the east of the house.

The house continues to give up its secrets. The lost sand-textured walls in the Egyptian Hall, a well under the south wall and, most recently, the discovery of wall paintings on the east staircase all demonstrate the remarkable depth (sometimes literal) of hidden facets of a building that has seen momentous events and promises to keep researchers engaged in unpeeling layers of history for many more years to come. In the final essay in this chapter, Rhiannon Clarricoates, of Hirst Conservation, provides a fascinating insight into the painstaking work of conservators revealing the wall paintings. This project brought together archival research, physical analysis and architectural studies in order to discover the identity of the subjects, the symbolism of the paintings and their place in the development of the house, while also looking at parallels elsewhere in works by the same artists.

Rigorous research and meticulous attention to detail at every stage are essential to preserve the fabric of this amazing building, which is so much more than bricks and mortar (or stonework and render). It has been a long journey from a building at risk to the restored grandeur that greets visitors today. Along the way we have had the pleasure of working with experts, and to know that traditional skills still exist in building, plasterwork, woodwork, metalwork and painting. To all those who dedicate their time to conservation and restoration, words cannot express sufficiently our appreciation and admiration of their skills. They have left the greatest testimony they could: a grand building beautifully restored.

following pages Stowe House in harmony with the landscape, pictured during restoration work in spring 2013. In the centre is the restored roundel, *Spring and Summer*, by James Lovell.

The Architect's View

JANE KENNEDY

The afternoon sun highlights details of the restored stonework.

In 1999 the Stowe House Preservation Trust (SHPT) was awarded a major Heritage Lottery Fund (HLF) grant and Purcell was appointed as its architect. The selection process was thorough and exemplary. The SHPT's first project manager, Bob Sharp, visited me in my office, met key staff, looked at work we had done elsewhere and came on a tour of Ely cathedral where I had been working for a number of years. Once appointed we were given a sizeable box of research papers and reports commissioned by the SHPT and largely undertaken by Inskip and Jenkins, who had looked after Stowe House and gardens for some years before. This included a four-volume conservation plan, folders of early illustrations of the house and detailed research on the pathology of the building.

The HLF grant had been offered for repairs to the North Front of the house and the conditions on which the grant was offered included increasing the number of visitors to the property and improving physical and intellectual access, as well as removing car parking from the forecourt and generally enhancing the appearance and approach to the house.

The North Front, some 120 metres long, was finished largely in render and this had cracked in many places, letting water into the soft red bricks underneath. We began research to identify a specification for a substitute render, bearing in mind the SHPT's requirement that it should not need maintenance for 75 years and thus a limewashed finish would be inappropriate. We did find small samples of what we believed to be the original lime render on the rear of the colonnades and this was analysed: it was made with a mildly hydraulic lime and local sand. Historic research told us that this render had lasted for about 90 years since 1780, and had been replaced in the nineteenth century with a Roman cement, which had

opposite below A replica herm on the North Front screen wall, representing the god Hermes who personifies eloquence and reason, the classical attributes of a teacher.

below left A comparison of substitute render finishes.

below right The Marble Saloon copper dome under repair.

failed leading to another cement render being applied. We set up tests and found a suitable sand quarried at Finmere, formerly part of the Stowe estate and only 5 kilometres away. Mixed with lime, it created a pleasing cream-coloured render that was specified for all subsequent work.

Other challenges in this project included identifying spaces around the site for replacement car parks, applying poultices to brickwork to remove harmful salts before re-rendering and researching local stone slates for the rear slopes of the colonnade roofs (and then locating experienced roofers who could lay them neatly). We went to Port Lympne in Kent to make copies of the herms for the outer North Front walls, and we made a full-size polystyrene mock-up of an urn designed to replace those lost from the parapet of the house. For the latter, we had to rely on *Country Life* photographs from 1914, which showed the urns from a distance. Enlarging these gave us an outline and we hoped we might find some of the originals reused in the gardens. Nothing matched and subsequently we discovered that they had been removed in the 1930s because they were crumbling and unsafe. The whole North Front contract had taken two years and was one of the last projects undertaken by the firm of Rattee and Kett from Cambridge.

Our next contracts were for the central pavilion and the Marble Saloon, which were again HLF funded. Work included removal of a 1960s' aluminium roof over the centre of the mansion to reveal the dome, and replacement of the lead roof coverings underneath. The temporary roof scaffold was lifted on by crane and was said to be the largest such structure ever to have been built in Britain. The dome is supported on timber beams, which were found to be quite badly rotted and had to be repaired in situ. The stud walls surrounding the Marble Saloon also underpinned an entire ring of cast-iron water tanks, some dating from the nineteenth century and others placed there by Stowe School. There was potential for catastrophic damage should the tanks have leaked into the timber and plaster walls, and the HLF grant enabled the School to excavate for and provide new water tanks in the grounds. A contractor was then commissioned to unbolt the tanks carefully and remove them piece by piece.

Externally we undertook stonework repairs using a Bath stone that was sympathetic in colour to the

many local stones used by the original builders. The research to find a matching stone included a trip into a mine near Bath and experiments with different strengths of diluted 'copperas' (an iron sulphate) to stain the stone. This technique had been employed in the eighteenth century to give the masonry a golden colour and perhaps to achieve uniformity across the variety of building stones. We used it to tone down the new sections of stone. Our philosophy was to replace any stone that was in danger of crumbling away or was dangerous, and to ensure that the crisp lines of the classical mouldings and architectural detail were retained. Some of the original work had been hastily done and was not always adequately fixed to the brick or rubble cores. In some places the facing stones were as little as 15 millimetres thick. We carefully repaired and conserved the frieze in the South Portico, which was then coloured to provide a consistent appearance.

Internally the Marble Saloon was scaffolded above the cornice and the decorative plasterwork was cleaned, repaired and limewashed. The triumphal procession scene had been damaged and we replaced missing limbs, spears and facial features. We also made sure that the trap door giving access to the internal sill, and which had formerly been used regularly by daring school boys, could be kept securely locked.

The work was finished when classical statuary was returned to the wall niches. This was organised by Tim Knox, then a trustee, who masterminded the acquisition of eight modern casts of classical figures and four copies of the 'Athéniennes', or torchères (as shown on p. 52). The lanterns over them all were replicas made to match those illustrated in a contemporary watercolour by the artist John Claude Nattes.

Turning to the exterior, a third phase of work saw masonry repairs carried out to the South Front, followed by re-roofing of the Library to the east of the Marble Saloon and internal repairs and redecoration of the ceiling. A failure of this roof in the early twentieth century had led to the removal of the roof trusses and a replacement of the covering with felt, which, over time, had caused damage to the delicate plaster ceiling underneath, loosening internal plasterwork. Fortunately, we were able to replicate the roof trusses on the matching pavilion to the west over the State Dining Room, and re-cover them in lead before carrying out extensive repairs to the plasterwork. During these works we found many traces of gold leaf and a decision was made to reinstate the original decoration to spectacular effect.

Stone replacements on the South Front.

The Library ceiling during gilding.

The new roof over the Library during construction.

The large scaffolding and temporary roof over the Marble Saloon during the second phase of restoration.

Further internal conservation has followed: the restoration of Vincenzo Valdrè's fine decorations in the State Music Room, the recreation of the decorative scheme in the Egyptian Hall, the reconstruction of the nineteenth-century appearance of the Blue Room with new silk damask to the walls, and careful repair and conservation of the William Kent ceiling in the North Hall. All our work has been supported by detailed historical research, carried out either within our own team or alongside SHPT staff. Trustees and others, including Michael Bevington from the School, and Martin Drury, former Director General of the National Trust (NT), have given considerable help, and critically reviewed our proposals. In addition, a scholarly approach has been taken to uncovering and documenting the painted decoration schemes following analysis by Patrick Baty.

An early decision was made to bring back the exterior of the house to its 'completion' around 1780–1800. To that end, the SHPT commissioned Cathy Fisher, a former colleague at Purcell who now lives in Los Angeles, to spend many months in the Huntington Library researching building records of those dates. Her research, which informed our approach and specifications, is now held by both the SHPT and the NT. Each project has involved detailed archaeological recording and the new information and reports from historians, archaeologists and conservators is extensive.

All contracts have included work to meet the practical needs of the SHPT's tenants, Stowe School. These have ranged from a careful upgrade of heating, wiring and fire protection systems for each project, to repairs to joinery and the strengthening and mending of floors. At an early stage, a lift was installed from the ground floor to the piano nobile and a small Welcome Centre with educational materials was provided for visitors, later replaced and remodelled as part of a further HLF grant to adapt the basement beneath the Marble Saloon. Programming 'opening up' works in school holidays, avoiding noise during exams, planning the contractors' working site for deliveries and access without risk to pupils, and designing scaffolds in the Marble Saloon and North Hall to give access for repairs while allowing the School and its visitors to function underneath have all involved detailed negotiations with the School, the SHPT, the events team, consultants and contractors. Many people have thus contributed to the success of the restoration and we will use much of what we have learned to inform future works.

Researching Decorative Schemes

PATRICK BATY

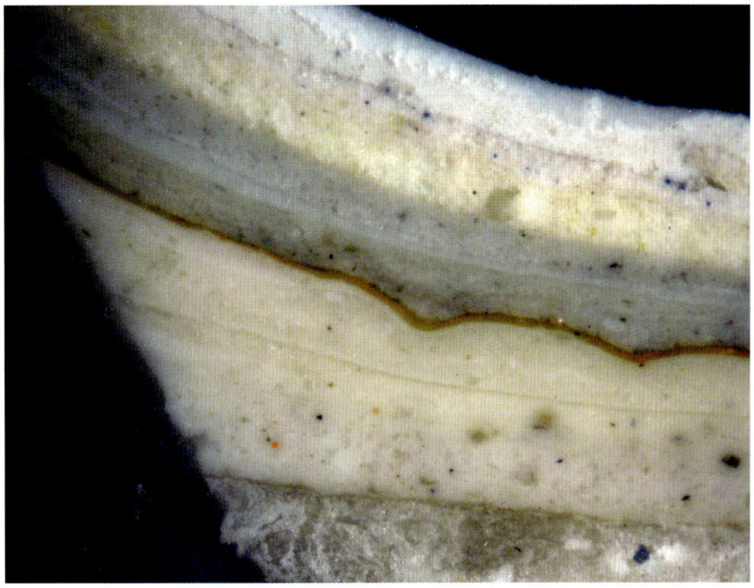

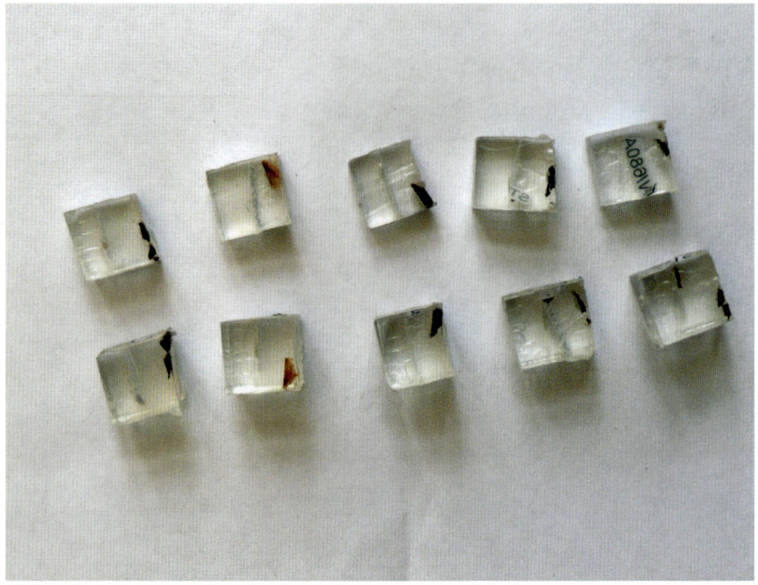

One of the rosettes in the Library: under the microscope, successive layers of paint show as different strata, often of varying thickness.

Paint samples prepared for examination.

The investigation of the painted surfaces at Stowe has demonstrated, if ever one needed proof, that such work is often the only way of learning about the changes that have taken place in a building. As important is the ability to suggest a date, or at least a period, for each of the decorative schemes. This has enabled the team working on the project to understand how each room appeared at different stages over the last 270 years. All this extra information can be gleaned when one seeks to find out what colours had been applied during a room's existence.

The process would appeal to those who enjoy jigsaws, for one has to take tiny samples from each representative element within a room and then try to build up a story. Check samples must also be taken, in order to ensure that repairs and later additions are identified. In complex rooms the numbers soon mount. It took 286 samples to establish how the Library appeared in 1805, our target date for the restoration of that room. This number was required because the initial samples showed that although the basic room structure was of the 1740s it had been partitioned in the 1760s. As the room is almost 23 metres long, each of the lower coffers along one side of the ceiling had to be sampled to see at what point the treatment changed. Analysis also showed that the decorative plasterwork on the ceiling had been augmented and gilded in the 1790s. When one considers that, on average, each sample takes an hour to process, the painstaking nature of the work becomes clear.

The samples are removed, each given a unique number and placed in small self-seal envelopes. Back in the workshop they are set in tiny blocks of quick-drying resin, which, when cured, are cut in half. The cut ends are polished using a succession of progressively finer wet and dry abrasive papers until a totally smooth and clear face results. All this is done by hand. At this stage, the samples can be examined under the microscope and photographed.

One must first confirm which samples display the full sequence and then, using a combination of logic, simple mathematics, pigment identification and a knowledge of precedent, fashion and the techniques of the early house painter, one can start to append a rough dateline to the sequence of paint layers. At this stage, any documentary or pictorial evidence can be considered, if it exists, to confirm or amend the hypothetical dating.

In the North Hall, an engraving from an 1845 issue of *The Illustrated London News* helped to date the filling in of the two sculpture niches that had been centred on each half of the south wall. The niches themselves had been revealed by paint analysis. At last the relevance of William Kent's laid-flat plan of the 1730s could be understood. We knew that the first scheme over the site of those niches must have been applied soon before 1845 and that the five schemes before that one were applied between *c.*1740 and *c.*1840. Already we had a rough 'repainting cycle' for the first hundred years.

Occasionally analysis provides tantalising glimpses of long-covered schemes. In the North Hall several samples had shown clear evidence of Kent's early painted designs in various areas but to remove all overlying paint in the hope of finding them complete and undamaged would be questionable. To restore them would also mean taking out the staircase to the Egyptian Hall, which dates from 1803, and reinstating the overmantel removed in 1788 and the chimney piece a few decades later. Paint analysis has shown us that the earliest state that the room can be returned to without a degree of conjecture or distortion is *c.*1840.

The Blue Room was one of the most complex of all the rooms at Stowe that have been examined to date. Paint sampling showed that the room contained elements from at least six different periods. Much of the joinery, the ceiling and cornice dated from the 1740s; the windows from the 1770s; the overdoors and wall plaster from about 1805, or soon after; the panel mouldings on the walls from the 1920s (since replaced); repairs to the east wall dated from the 1960s to 1970s and the chimney piece and skirting fascia were installed in 1988. It was only when the samples from each element were compared that the puzzle could be assembled, but it took 183 samples, that is, over four weeks' work.

Photographs of the room, taken in 1870 and 1921, confirmed details of the disposition of gold and provided information on the blue silk wallcovering, which has recently been rewoven. The degree of subtlety of the 1860s' scheme, which has been recreated, was quite exceptional. Paint analysis showed that two different types of gold leaf had been applied to the ceiling. The greater part of it was gilded with a purer, reddish-gold and the picking-out was in a greener, less pure, gold. Some of the gilding was burnished and some was not. This sort of attention to detail is usually seen on only the finest furniture.

In the State Dining Room something of the playfulness of the 1740s' decoration was revealed.

Her Majesty Queen Victoria's departure from Stowe House, *The Illustrated London News*, 25 January 1845.

William Kent's laid-flat plan of the North Hall, 1730.

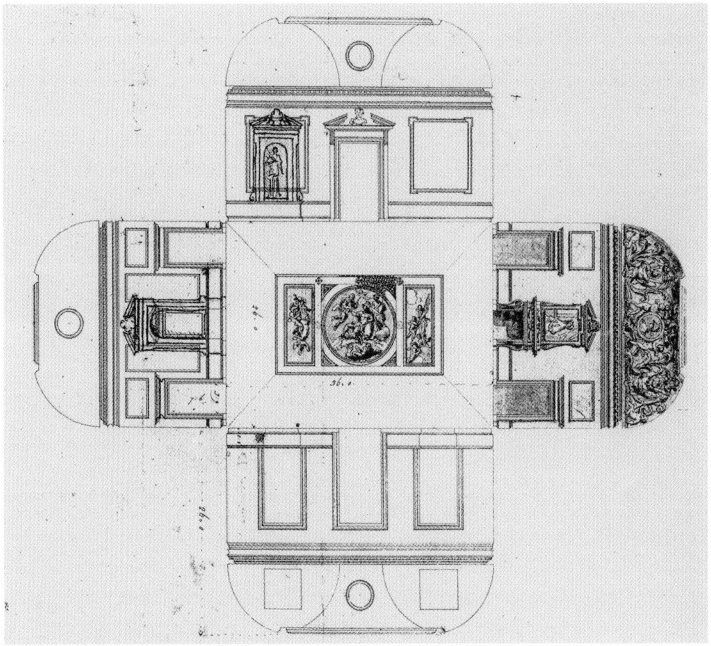

The Blue Room, 1921.

Analysis showed that the 'pebble-dashed' frieze had originally been gilded in order to catch the glint of candlelight. It must have sparkled at night. Sadly, this and much of the other gilding was painted over at a later date presenting a more sober appearance. It could also be shown that the window architraves still retained their original paint and gilding from the 1770s in spite of nearly a century as a school dining room.

A significant lesson that has been learnt at Stowe is that the information gained by examining one room can very often help with other rooms. The same paint or combination of pigments can be spotted and therefore another clue is given to the dating of schemes. The analysis of the paint at Stowe has provided us with an enormous amount of information about the house, its development and decoration. It has also contributed greatly to the decision-making process.

left Gilding in progress in the Blue Room.

right Gilding to the Library ceiling: the end result of painstaking research and skilled conservation.

Textile Recreations for the Blue Room

ANNABEL WESTMAN

The completed Blue Room, with restored oak floor, new blue silk damask panels, curtains and gold leaf decoration.

Over the years, the Blue Room has had nine names and is an amalgam of several different schemes that reflected its changing use.[1] The current name dates from the 1860s when the room was hung with 'blue satin damask', as recorded in the 1871 inventory. Little is known of its earlier incarnations although throughout most of the eighteenth century it was hung with fabric, either crimson or green velvet, or tapestries with designs by David Teniers. Only during the first half of the nineteenth century, when the room was fitted with mahogany bookcases and became known as the Ante-Library, and after the 1922 sale when the blue damask panels were sold and the walls painted blue for classroom use, have the walls been exposed.

In the 2014 restoration, the decision was made to return to the 1860 scheme as the one best recorded and least disruptive architecturally and where the later history of the house could successfully be told. The gilded and painted ceiling was subsequently restored to a scheme researched by Patrick Baty and a search was begun to find a suitable damask for the wall panels and curtains. With nothing surviving of the original furnishings, a few black and white photographs dating from the 1870s and 1920s proved invaluable as the only visual evidence available. The images showed a floral damask design on the walls, curtains and seat furniture that, although not clear enough to copy, was sufficiently visible to appreciate its scale and repeat.

Fortunately, the fabric was described in the two twentieth-century sale catalogues. The 1921 publication referred to it as a 'very handsome blue and silver flowered satin damask', while the second, produced the following year, noted that the 'blue ground silk damask' was 'of silvered festoons, musical and pastoral emblems and floral design'. In the ensuing research, both French and British archives were explored as, in 1860, the ability to purchase French fabrics had just been made considerably easier by the signing of the Cobden Treaty, which removed the import duty from silk products. However, most of the potential patterns studied were too small for the room and could not be enlarged successfully without destroying the design. The closest match was eventually discovered in the Warner Textile Archive in Braintree, Essex, the largest textile archive in the public domain. With the reference name 'Sherwood', it was dated 1899 but its floral design was very much mid-nineteenth century in conception and practically identical in scale. It also

The Blue Room, 1921.

The Blue Room in 2017, with a copy of *Richard Grenville, 2nd Earl Temple*, by Allan Ramsay, 1762.

could be described as 'with festoons' although it lacked the additional 'musical and pastoral emblems'.

With the design now in hand, colour was the other factor to identify in order to fit the documentary description of blue satin ground and silver/white pattern. Close attention was paid to the blue paint of the ceiling with the knowledge that turquoise blues in textiles were popular at this time. A perfect match was found, again in the Warner Textile Archive: a silk damasquette entitled 'Hindley' woven in blue and silver by the British company, Keith & Co., around 1860 for Hindley & Son, one of the leading decorators of the day. Like the original description, this fabric had a satin ground so the weave structure, with its twill figure in the pattern, and the colours were copied as typical of the 1860s. It was woven by Richard Humphries Weaving Ltd, based in Sudbury, where Keith & Co. had also had a factory until 1868.[2]

In fixing the fabric to the walls, tack-hole evidence revealed that the fabric had originally been attached under the 'carved gold and white, beaded and rope pattern borders',[3] and that woven braid had been used around the overmantel mirror and door frames. The wood mouldings had been sold in the 1922 sale and cheaper versions put up in their place. These later models were removed and copies made of the originals from the photographs, in plaster rather than wood, which was more economical to replicate. As the fabric now had to be fixed within the borders, braid was specially woven from a contemporary pattern in two colours to match the fabric, and applied to mask the tack heads as well as around the mirror and doors.

No attempt was made in the restoration to refurnish the room and recreate the crowded appearance seen in the early photographs and backed up by descriptions in the documentation. Nor has a carpet been replaced, listed in the 1871 inventory as a bordered Persian carpet with rug, which by 1921 had become a 'Brown Ground Hand-Made Tapestry Carpet' with 'flowered pile hearthrug, with black fringe'. The SHPT had previously restored the floor, replacing an inappropriate laminate surface with beautifully worked and authentic oak boards in 2013. The only other items that were recreated were the two pairs of window curtains once trimmed with cord and made to match the wall hangings, suspended from brass poles with finials and rings. The original curtains were longer but this detail was judged impractical given the current use of the room by Stowe School, although the 'Four pairs of handsome silk embrace tassels' have been replaced, based on an example from the 1860s, to complete the ensemble.

above 'Sherwood' design, 1899 (width 53 cm x vertical pattern repeat 75 cm), found in the Warner Textile Archive.

centre Detail of the specially woven braid with the re-created plaster borders.

below Detail of the double-tassel curtain tie-backs made from a design *c.*1860.

The Egyptian Hall

JOHN MADDISON

The Egyptian Hall looking to the west, its walls with the pronounced batter as recorded in Dominique Vivant-Denon's drawing of the temple of Hathor at Dendera.

The steps of Sir John Vanburgh's North Portico span a cobbled carriage route that sweeps round to the ground floor of the house where service quarters and family rooms of a comfortable scale underlie the magnificent spaces of the piano nobile. In the nineteenth century, visitors alighting from their carriages in the porte cochère beneath the steps would enter these ground-floor rooms via the Egyptian Hall.

Built in 1803 by the 1st Marquess of Buckingham, the Egyptian Hall was inspired by the engravings of Baron Dominique Vivant-Denon's *Travels in Upper and Lower Egypt* of 1802. Denon, an antiquary and accomplished artist, was one of several specialists, or *savants*, who accompanied Napoleon Bonaparte on his campaigns in Egypt. His two large folios put before the public the most extensive and accurate illustrations of Egyptian art yet published and started a widespread fashion for neo-Egyptian decoration of which this little entrance hall at Stowe is an exceptionally early instance. As the 1820 edition of the Stowe guidebook recorded:

The Egyptian Hall is fitted up from Denon's designs of the remains in the interior of one of the small temples of

The ceiling of the Egyptian Hall features a representation of the zodiac design from the temple at Dendera.

Tintyra. The ceiling is vaulted, and ornamented with the celebrated Egyptian Zodiac found in the ceiling of that temple. The walls are decorated with hieroglyphics and various designs copied from the Temples and Sepulchres of Tintyra and Thebes.[1]

The temple of Hathor at Dendera – or Tintyra as Denon knew it – is one of the finest of the later Egyptian temples (110 BC–AD 68) and Denon's engravings of its principal façade and carved reliefs are among the most striking images in his publication.

The architect of the Egyptian Hall is not known. Sir John Soane made clear that it was not his work and he refers to no one else, apart from his patron, so it has to be assumed that the 1st Marquess worked up the scheme with his builders. The pronounced slope, or batter, of its side walls and the various Egyptian motifs in the plasterwork come from Denon, and the overall plan, a rectangle with a shallow apse behind a column screen, is typical of contemporary neoclassicism.

The complete contents of the Egyptian Hall, including its paintings, the sarcophagus-stove that occupied the apse and the crouching sphinxes that flanked the staircase, were sold in the Stowe sale of 1921. The only visual records of the room's original appearance are two monochrome watercolours painted by John Claude Nattes shortly after its completion in 1805. These views were clearly faithful records of its general appearance but treated the decorations as generic neoclassical figure groups of a kind found in many country houses of the time. For this reason they cannot be relied upon in a reconstruction of the decoration. The 'Egyptian zodiac' on the ceiling is not shown and may not have been completed by the time of the artist's visit.

The restoration of the Egyptian Hall began with the repair of its plasterwork and the removal of a partition in the apse that had formed a telephone call box. Following an initial research paper by Hettie Dix of the Stowe House Preservation Trust (SHPT), between 2013 and 2014 I researched in detail the

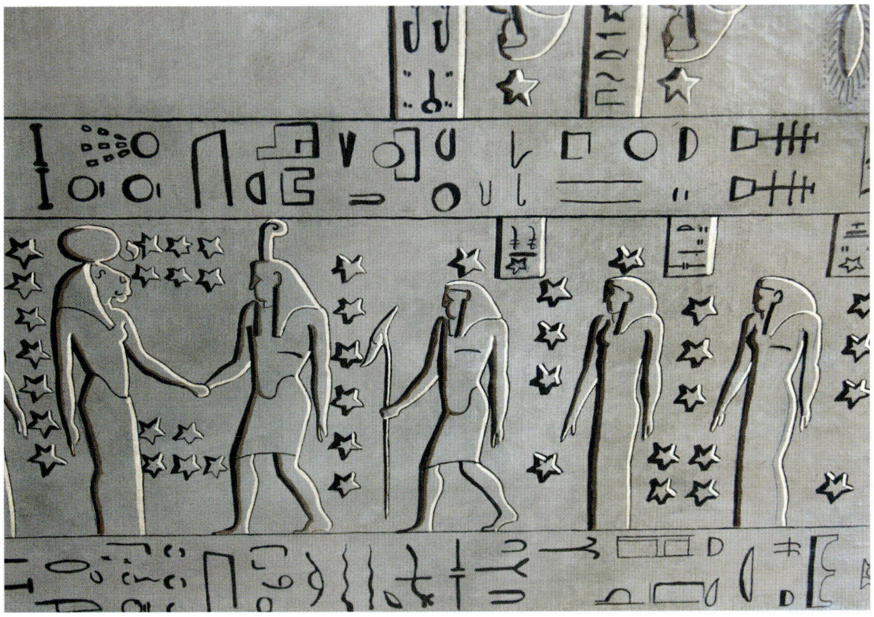
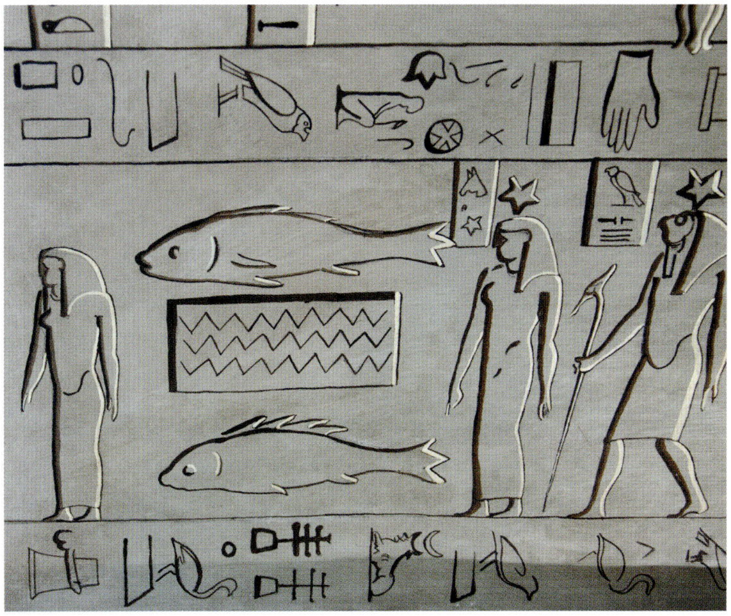

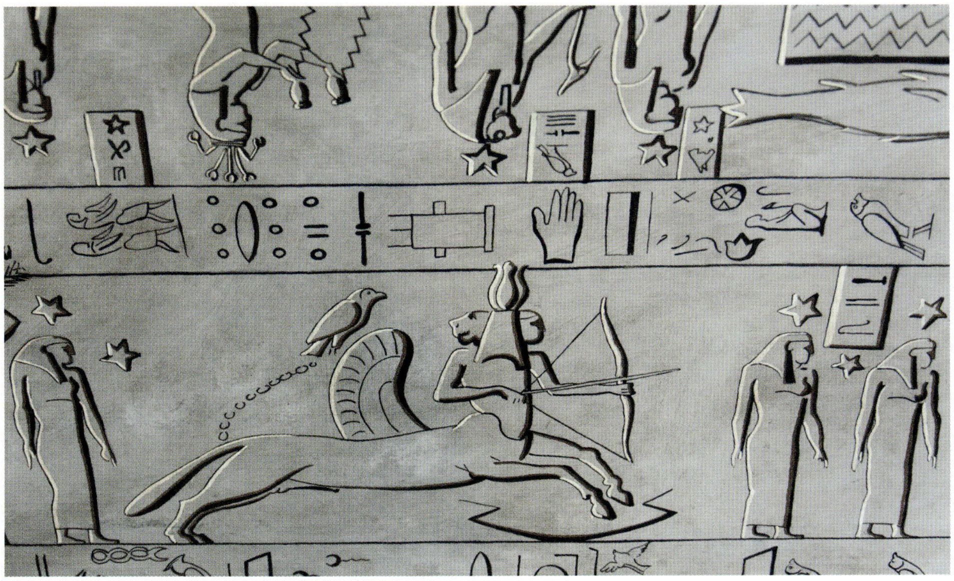

clockwise from top right A detail from the zodiac frieze in the centre of the Egyptian Hall ceiling; a sacrifice to Khonsu, the moon god; the goddess Hathor seated on a throne decorated with papyrus and lotus stems facing the enthroned figure of the ibis-headed deity Thoth; a detail from the zodiac frieze; the goddess Satet; a detail from the zodiac frieze; and the barque of Ra flanked by two crouching figures of Anubis (*centre*).

A monochrome watercolour of the Egyptian Hall, by John Claude Nattes, *c.*1805.

painted figure subjects of the ceiling and walls, which I then composed and executed.

The approach was to select compositions, individual figures and devices from Denon to fill the various plaster recesses and frames that once contained the originals. Accurate replication of the original decoration was not possible but it made sense to follow Denon's drawings as closely as possible and to consult other early nineteenth-century painted decoration at Stowe. The scheme of 2014 is therefore a product of our time that has an informed historical relationship with the lost originals.

The 1st Marquess and his painters had a limited understanding of Egyptian myth. Hieroglyphs were completely unintelligible to modern Europeans until Jean-François Champollion published his translation of the Rosetta Stone in 1822. In the new work of 2013–14 the painted scenes were therefore put together with an eye to making satisfactory compositions consistent with early nineteenth-century decorative traditions rather than anything more archaeologically correct.

The 6-metre ceiling canvas copies the two central registers in Denon's engraving of a sky chart on the ceiling of the hypostyle hall or portico of the main temple at Dendera.

As the Egyptian Hall derives very little natural light from the windows that open onto the porte cochère the 1st Marquess made a virtue of the gloom. A large lens, magnifying the flame of an oil lamp, was set in an ornamental plaster surround above the door to the main ground-floor corridor. This sun-disk was the only artificial illumination. The sarcophagus stove, fed and stoked from the room behind the apse, provided gentle – if not Egyptian – warmth in winter, and a little borrowed daylight from adjacent rooms gave mysterious illumination to two stained-glass panels matching the painted canvases of the mural recesses. The new glass panels were painted by Dan Humphries of Holy Well Glass, from my cartoons.

The small staircase between two recumbent sphinxes on the east side of the room leads up to the North Hall allowing visitors to enjoy an instructive comparison between the classical grandeur of the piano nobile and the seemingly more archaic Egyptian entrance, which lay beneath like a recently discovered tomb in the Valley of the Kings. That such a comparison was intended is reinforced by the appearance of zodiac subjects in the ceilings of both rooms.

Lighting Up Stowe House

JOHN DARLINGTON AND NICK MORRIS

The State Music Room chandelier, faithfully reproduced from photographic evidence.

Expert advice warns of the difficulties of lighting historic buildings to acceptable modern standards without distorting the architecture.[1] Historically, lighting generally had three functions: symbolic, ostentation and task. Creating a high level of task lighting can result in the first two being lost, yet these are the very purposes that, in a house like Stowe, we should seek to replicate. Simple cornice lighting shows decorated ceilings to advantage but is not historically accurate and so the challenge is to light the interiors in such a way as to enhance understanding of the architecture while complying with current standards of illumination for work and safety. At Stowe, we faced a further dilemma in the lack of clear evidence for the lighting that must have been a feature of such grand rooms within the house.

In the case of the State Music Room, our own records proved invaluable. Research showed that, in the eighteenth century, a single chandelier had illuminated the room from the centre of Vincenzo Valdrè's *Dance of the Hours*. This had been sold and replaced later by five individual chandeliers. The 1848 sale catalogue listed the disposal of the chandelier but, in a surprising twist of fate, the same chandelier had been purchased back by the 3rd Duke and found its way to the Blue Room, where, in the early twentieth century, it had been photographed (see p.89). The trail was confirmed, the evidence compelling and the case made for a replica to be commissioned using documentary photographs. However, things are rarely that simple and, during restoration of the *Dance of the Hours*, doubt arose as to whether the painting had initially been pierced to allow the introduction of a chandelier or whether the chandelier was a late addition. Further meticulous research revealed that the canvas had been cut back to give space for wires and a chain and, once again, the case was clear. Using the later photographs from the Blue Room, an exact copy was commissioned from a specialist company that manufactures replica period lighting and its work now graces the centre of the room. The controversy was not quite over though, as considerable debate ensued over the presence, or not, in the eighteenth century of a central boss that appeared to be illustrated in some images. Once again, comprehensive research was conducted of the painted surface with the conclusion that, in all probability, the centre of the painting had once been covered by a boss symbolising a radiating sun, and that feature was added.

The Library posed a completely different challenge. Trustees and advisors were conscious that, here, lighting could not be separated from function and furnishing or from how the School would like it to operate. It was important that the Library should not feel daunting or intimidating to younger pupils. Consideration was given to using 'uplighters' for their positive architectural presence as furniture, but, in the end, 'task' lighting was selected for the desks and bookcases with cornice lighting to highlight the beautiful gilded ceiling. However, we were all intrigued by two eighteenth-century depictions: a watercolour by Joseph Nash and an engraving that appeared to show pendant lighting of a type that no one had encountered anywhere else. Other than these images,

below The Library in 1809, artist unknown, signed 'ES'.

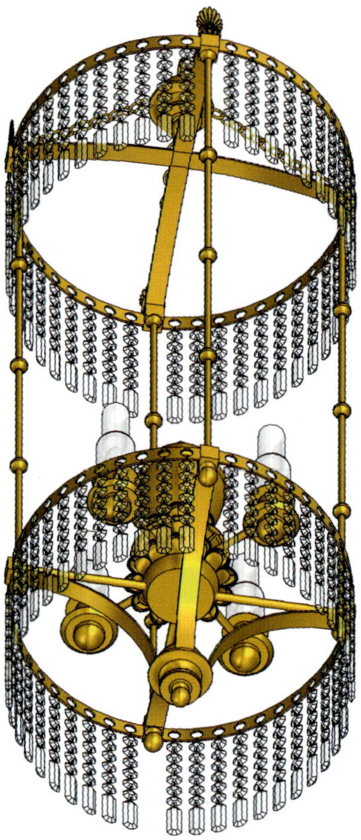

left to right

The sketch design, a final trial mock-up to assess proportions, and the completed lantern in the Library.

A trial of atmospheric lighting in the Egyptian Hall.

there was no evidence for any lighting in the room apart from references to ormolu chandeliers and glass lustres in the 1839 inventory.

The two depictions were compelling and both appeared to show a cylindrical lantern with a central bowl that might have held kolsa oil feeding wicks to candle-shaped lights around the base. Research into studies of eighteenth-century lighting and reference to images of many country houses failed to reveal anything comparable so the bold decision was taken to attempt to replicate the lanterns as shown in the watercolour and engraving. However, as both were distorted by perspective, it was difficult to judge the size of the lanterns or their height by comparison with other features in the room.

We decided to proceed by 'trial and error'. Our first attempts fell way short of the mark but, gradually, through a process of sketching by Jonathan Foyle (then Director of World Monuments Fund Britain), trial mock-ups and visual reference, suitable dimensions were established and it was possible to commission lanterns from the same company that was making the State Music Room replica chandelier.

In the Egyptian Hall, there was even less to work on when considering suitable lighting. In reality, the space was probably intended to have a certain element of gloom, as would befit the Egyptian temple that it represented. However, this would not meet modern safety considerations. For a while, uplighters were trialled, but eventually it was decided to adopt a sympathetic modern lighting arrangement, created as a bespoke installation by a leading designer of systems for historic interiors.

The process of recreating authentic lighting to meet the needs of a twenty-first-century academic institution while preserving the appearance of the building and allowing visitors to see the interiors as their creators intended has been a particular challenge. Throughout, we have been governed by the principles of rigorous scholarship and reversibility, supplemented by confidant curatorship. The State Music Room and the Library prove what can be done through pains-taking research and trial designs with the support of skilled craftspeople. The results more than justify the effort of many, but without the support of a generous donor, none of this would have been possible.

The Temple-Grenvilles as Collectors

ANNA McEVOY

The 1922 sale underway in the Marble Saloon.

The 1922 sale poster.

The beauty of Stowe today is in the man-made landscape strewn with unusual follies and the bombastic ducal mansion with its well-preserved and delicate interiors. What Stowe is missing is the huge collection of items that once populated the estate. The original collection, amassed over 150 years, was sold in the infamous sale of 1848, after the 2nd Duke of Buckingham and Chandos ran up debts of £1.5 million. The sale, for which it was said people came from far and wide to witness the downfall of a great man, raised a mere £75,000. The estate was shut up and the 2nd Duke never went back to Stowe. His son, almost impoverished by his father, returned as the 3rd Duke in 1861, and tried his utmost to reinstate the family's name and fortune. Ultimately, the family fell victim to the circumstances of the age: by 1921, with the heir, the Master of Kinloss, having been killed at the beginning of the First World War and his brother unable to raise enough money to keep such an estate running, it was sold. All the contents – items that had not been sold in 1848, or which had been bought by the 3rd Duke at the sale or acquired during his time as governor of Madras – were part of the sales lot. At the eleventh hour the estate was saved from being dismantled by Harry Shaw, a Hampshire-based property developer, who wanted to present this treasure house to the nation as a gift. Without an endowment, neither the government nor the National Trust was able to accept it. Within nine months, and having trialled various schemes to keep the estate intact, he had to sell it again. This time, in order to make back the money that he had originally lost, he stripped out most of the fixtures and fittings that could be moved – chimney pieces, ceiling paintings and wall hangings – as well as the accumulated artefacts. Within the first three days of the 1922 sale, Shaw had recouped the money he had spent on buying the estate, and therefore made a profit from the subsequent sales: ironically, that would have been enough to cover an endowment.

What of Stowe's family, the Temple-Grenvilles, as collectors? Did they seek to rival their peers, such as the Dukes of Devonshire, Bedford or Marlborough? The answer is, probably not. While the Marquess of Buckingham had inherited the magnificent Thomas Astle collection of manuscripts in 1804 and had added to this subsequently, the sale of this collection in 1849 was considered rather poignant: indeed, the beautiful Gothic Library created by Sir John Soane was built specially to hold this unique collection and was now bereft of it. In the State Drawing Room had hung Old Masters – Tintoretto, Nicolas Poussin, Albrecht Dürer and Peter Paul Rubens – and one room was dedicated to a large collection of works by Rembrandt. At one point, there may have been a statue gallery that ran from the Laocoön in the North Hall (itself purchased from the great Fonthill sale of 1823) through the Marble Saloon, with its statues collected on the Grand Tour in the 1770s, out to the South Portico niches housing colossal female statues. Was it a conscious collection or a happy accident?

It was the 1st Duke who might be described as a collector, through his creation of a museum in his mother's Ménagerie, a beautiful glass-fronted temple near the main mansion. The 1838 guidebook describes 'about a thousand specimens of stuffed Birds, Animals, Fishes, and Reptiles', and the Duke purchased some dramatic examples of taxidermy. The violent interplay between predatory species was particularly popular. However, it is the 'Buckingham collection of mineralogy and geology, containing more than six thousand specimens' – sold for £68 in 1848 – that gives the first indication of a collector's eye. In the diaries compiled as he explored the Mediterranean for two years, the 1st Duke writes with much detail about the geological landscape and discoveries using the language of an expert, no doubt educated by the leading geologists of the day whom he invited to curate the collection. Access to the collection was by special permission – as opposed to his more open estate and house – suggesting it was a place of study rather than of one-upmanship.

What is the motivation behind any collector or collection? To compete with others? To exhibit one's taste and knowledge, not to mention wealth? To justify one's position in society? To be seen as a leader of architectural and artistic fashion? These intentions are perhaps reinforced by the opening of Stowe to the public. The building of New Inn in 1717, as a travellers' rest before and after a walk round the grounds and house, dates Stowe as one of the earliest tourist attractions in Britain. Guidebooks, printed and sold locally, date from 1744 and run, with updated versions, until 1838, documenting the evolution of the gardens, the house and the collection. They allow us to track when items were purchased, placed, moved or disposed of, culminating in the infamous sale of 1848. The 1839 and 1871 house inventories help to fill in gaps and, more intriguingly, enable us to see the domestic as well as the designer items: sheets, stools, lamps, beds, carpets and so on.

So what did Stowe lose through its two great sales? We are lucky enough to have sales catalogues to help us gauge the extent of this fall – the 1848 catalogue was reprinted soon after the sale by an entrepreneurial Victorian, Henry Rumsey Forster,

The Ménagerie, an early museum, is now used as the School shop: a photograph taken in the 1890s (*left*), and the interior of the dome, painted by Vincenzo Valdrè (*right*).

The restored original of the *Dance of the Hours* ready for reinstatement.

listing the buyers of each object – and the contents, both in amount and finery, are eye-watering. There were hundreds of classical artefacts gleaned from Rome, many of them obtained in the sale by Forster personally, such as the Marine Venus originally from the baths of Agrippa, an antique chimera from near the Villa Adriana, a statue of a Roman senator from Herculaneum, and an antique Roman sarcophagus found on the road to Tivoli. There were also items with a well-known background story – the State Bed with yellow silk curtains and hangings and a lining of crimson silk, and the State Chair made for Queen Victoria's visit – as well as objects from other sales like those at Fonthill, in Wiltshire, and the Doge's Palace, in Venice; the contents of the famous Stowe geological museum, including the Mary Anning *Plesiosaurus Dolichodeirus* fossil; a collection of telescopes made by Mr Dollond; and the celebrated Chandos portrait of Shakespeare, thought to be the work of Richard Burbage. We should not forget the lock of Queen Mary's hair that was taken from her coffin, or Napoleon's supper tray and a pair of steel spades with plush-covered handles used by Victoria and Albert to plant trees at Stowe in 1845.

While, with hindsight, we may lament the loss of these treasures from one house, it is only part of the historic sense of recycling – or the result of aristocratic coveting – which adds to each item's story and value. Sometimes this recycling comes full circle.

This is seen in the recent rediscovery of the group, *The Laocoön*, a large bronze statue depicting a Trojan priest, Laocoön, fighting off a sea serpent sent by the gods to attack him and his two sons. The original Roman marble sculpture, rediscovered in

1506, was copied several times over the centuries and one version was purchased for William Beckford for Fonthill Abbey. Beckford sold the estate when he ran out of money – a familiar tale – enabling the newly created Duke of Buckingham and Chandos to buy the bronze (among many other valuable items), via a dealer, to display in the North Hall that William Kent had created 100 years earlier. The statue is described in the 1832 guidebook and is also depicted in an *Illustrated London News* image of Queen Victoria and Prince Albert leaving Stowe House at the end of their three-day visit in January 1845 (see p. 85). After

Ceiling paintings on plaster in the State Music Room survived because they could not be removed for sale.

its sale in 1848, it ended up at Hamilton Palace, in Lanarkshire, home to the Dukes of Hamilton, and was sold again in 1919.

Similarly, the central ceiling painting in the beautiful State Music Room, Vincenzo Valdrè's *Dance of the Hours*, was sold in 1922 and came up for sale again in 1978, but funds could not be raised for Stowe to purchase it. A copy on hardboard was made to fill the gap, but by sheer serendipity soon after the room's restoration in 2012 the original painting was found in a London townhouse. The owners generously allowed the painting to be bought by the Stowe House Preservation Trust (SHPT), and after a year of painstaking restoration it was returned to its original position, 230 years after it had first been created. In the same vein, the South Front steps are now protected by the original 1791 lead lions, returned to Stowe after their 90-year holiday in Stanley Park in Blackpool.

So, after all that, what collection is there now to see at Stowe House? The North Hall has two lovely marble reliefs created 100 years apart, which could not be sold in the 1922 sale and therefore remain. In the Library there are the fitted mahogany bookcases, installed in the 1790s, as well as the elaborate marble chimney pieces, which may have been in the room since it began life as a ballroom in the 1740s. With the exception of Valdrè's ceiling painting mentioned above, the beautifully hand-painted State Music Room retained all its artwork as this had been painted straight onto the plaster, an attempt at Roman fresco work.

So much for fixtures and fittings, but what of the gilded furniture, jewelled trinkets, travel mementoes, historic manuscripts and books, personalised dinner services, engraved glassware and silk curtains? Since the creation of Stowe School in 1923, when 99 boys arrived at an empty 400-room house, items have been given or sold to Stowe to help illustrate the rise and fall of the estate and family. These have come via auctions, descendants of the family, Old Stoics and serendipity. They include part of the famous Stowe dinner service, glassware, silverware and paintings of family members, as well as a cherished locket and painted miniatures.

In 1982, following the sale of a collection of stuffed birds assembled by John Hall and donated to the School by Patrick Hall, a fund was set up to enable the purchase of historic items as well as to provide bursaries for pupils and help with the visual arts. Since 1982, we have been indebted to the Hall Bequest Trust for funding acquisitions that allow a greater understanding of the artistic richness of Stowe.

Our 'Lost Treasures of Stowe' project seeks to discover the whereabouts of Stowe artefacts, not with the aim of repatriating them, but to create a photographic record so that we can imagine the splendours of the State Rooms. We need these to help us envisage the life and opulence of the family, to appreciate the individual tastes of each owner and to understand the fascinating development of Stowe. We are now in a position to start our own collection based on availability, size and provenance to help us tell the history of Stowe to future generations of pupils and visitors.

Lost treasures of Stowe on display in the Discovery Centre.

1921 sale
A pair of grape-scissors
Napoleon's supper-tray, consisting of a circular soup-tureen, cover, and liner, four dishes with classical friezes around the edges and winged figures, stands for pepper and salt, in a mahogany case
A ball in Venice – (Tintoretto)
A classical landscape, with a bridge and figures – (Claude)
A beautiful ancient oak chest, richly carved with figures and Gothic panels – from the Jerusalem Chamber at Westminster Abbey
A lock of the hair of Queen Mary, taken from the corpse at St. Mary's Church, Bury, when her coffin was opened
Portrait of Henry VIII, in a rich slashed dress, with hat and feather – (Holbein)
The celebrated Chandos portrait of Shakespeare, presumed to be the work of Burbage, the first actor of Richard III
372 15 0
elephant – a copy from that in the Piazza di Minerva, at Rome
An elegant antique group of three female figures, supporting a vase, on a truncated column of grey marble
The Apollo Belvidere – a small copy, in marble
16 0 0
A Roman bust with drapery of alabaster
5 0 0
An antique Roman sarcophagus, with reliefs of cupids hunting wild animals upon the feet and ends
16 16 0
A telescope, by Dollond
A handsome sofa, with carved rosewood frame and stuffed seat, the three back cushions, two pillows and two bolsters covered with crimson satin damask
325 10 0
A large easy chair, with stuffed back and cushion, covered with richly flowered green silk damask
22 11 6
7 17 6

The Medici Lions: Conserving Lead Statuary

RUPERT HARRIS

opposite Guardians once more, the Medici lions back in place at the foot of the South Front steps.

The west lion at Stanley Park in Blackpool, tilting forward and supported on a makeshift cement prop, with its right paw raised on a sphere.

The Flemish sculptor John Van Nost the Elder came to London with William III in 1689. Equipped with superior lead-working skills, he started a business in Piccadilly where he produced lead garden statues in considerable numbers.

Other artists' yards followed, including those of Andrew Carpenter and Henry Cheere. Cheere was a very successful sculptor, specialising in carved stone funerary monuments, busts and fire surrounds; he trained his brother, John, and in about 1739 helped John to establish his own practice by purchasing Van Nost's statuary yard, stock and moulds (some of which may have originated with Arnold Quellin), and possibly Carpenter's moulds also.

British lead sculptures of the seventeenth and eighteenth centuries were either produced from moulds taken directly from antique marbles or from new models that referenced the antique and other artists' work, often borrowing elements of a sculptural composition and using these to depict a different allegory or figure.

The Stowe lions are almost certainly from the studio of John Cheere, as the sculptures display the very characteristic hallmark of fine after-cast, chased detail seen on many other works known to originate from his studio. We have identified only two other casts of one of the Stowe lions: at Charlton Park, Wiltshire (this lion's tail has been modified), and at Staunton Harold Hall, Leicestershire. Cheere was almost certainly the maker of all these.

Each sculpture was made as a one piece lost-wax casting in lead, with the refractory plaster core and iron armature remaining inside; the armature projected from the sculpture base and was used to attach the sculpture to the square top stone of its limestone base.

On first inspection, the lead lions in Stanley Park in Blackpool appeared to be in good structural condition. However, the west lion had had an additional cement support placed under the raised right front leg. This suggested that there was a potential problem with the internal armature within this leg or that the lion had started to lean due to the fixings having worked loose over time. The possibility of this lion having moved on its base and being slightly distorted was borne out by the fact that the rear paws were supported by built-up cement pads. The east lion sat more closely to the plinth stone and did not have additional cement supports (see p. 109). When comparing the two lions in profile it could be seen

that the body and head of the west lion had dropped towards the front.

The surface of both lions was found to be in reasonable condition but, as the public regularly climbed upon them, the patina, particularly on their backs, had become polished. The remainder of the surface had a typical lead oxide and carbonate dull grey patination with darker brown areas of lead dioxide, the latter being a phenomenon that has started to occur only in the past 20 years (thought to be the result of changes in the composition of air-borne pollution). There was little graffiti, despite the surface being particularly vulnerable to vandalism. The base stones to which the lions were attached, assumed to be the original top plinth stones from Stowe, were heavily weathered but remained serviceable.

The lions were safely removed while still attached to the top plinth stones and transported to our workshop, where they were separated from the stones. As expected, this revealed small, corroded iron fixing dowels. Tiny samples of paint found in the recessed modelling were analysed. The results showed that the lions had been painted with oil paint at least eight times. The paints were all based on lead white, so these decorations must have been applied before the 1940s. The sculptures would originally have been painted to simulate stone, as is the case with the majority of Cheere's and other eighteenth-century lead-makers' garden sculpture.

Patches were cut to allow access to the interior.

Both lions now have a new stainless-steel armature.

The patches were then reinstated, initially by tack welding.

The cast tail end, before being lead burnt into place.

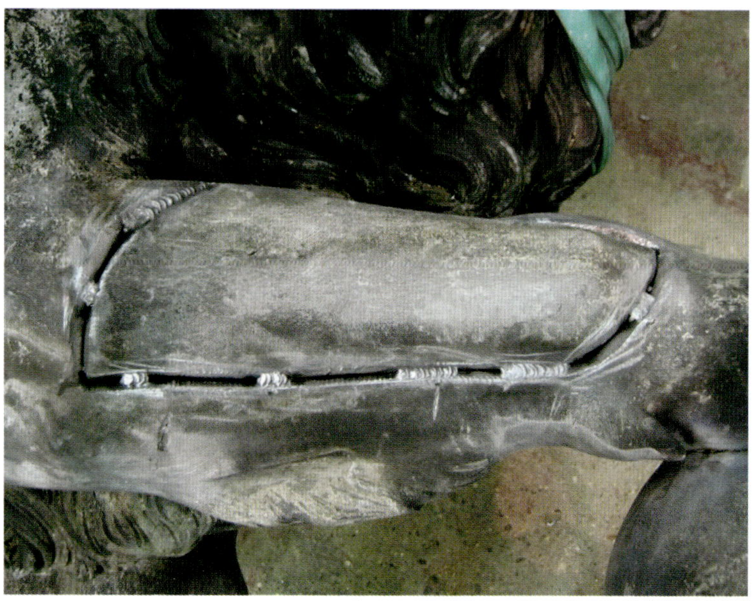

The lions being loaded onto the flatbed for their return to Stowe.

Secure reinstatement of the original lions at Stowe in April 2013.

Once in the studio, an inspection was made of the armatures of both lions to assess their condition; from this, recommendations were made for work seen as necessary to ensure the sculptures' survival. The west lion required correction of its tilt, due to the failure of the armature. Patches were cut in both lions to enable the removal of internal core and failed iron armature bars. The core material consisted of a mixture of sand and plaster; if not extracted, this and the corroded iron armature could promote damage in the future. The slumped back and other areas of the west lion were rectified by reworking the original lead to correct its form and a new armature, constructed from Grade 316 stainless steel, was fixed into the interior of each lion, in both the body and the base area. The patches were lead burned back into place by first being tacked and then the whole join lead burned; finally, the join was worked back and finished. A new tail end was moulded in wax and cast in lead to replace the missing piece of the east lion's tail and security fixings were added to the base armature of both lions. Following the completion of all repairs, the surface was treated with casein-based paints to disguise the worked areas, which will slowly wear off to be replaced by a natural patina. The two lead lions were then packed onto pallets and transported to Stowe on their original stone bases, which were fixed back onto their original plinths.

Material options for replicating the lions for Stanley Park were considered. There are no alternative metals that lend themselves to this, as neither bronze, nor aluminium nor iron would be aesthetically suitable. Polyester resin reinforced glass fibre was an option, as this can be coloured and imbedded with pigments to simulate lead very well. However, as a substitute material, resin copies are often frowned upon and are perceived as substandard. New casts in lead honour the original sculptures' material and can have a substantial stainless-steel armature built within them, which can be firmly secured to the existing plinths, making theft very difficult. In light of this, and taking into account the need for Blackpool Council to be in a position to justify the loan of the originals to Stowe, it was agreed that new lead casts would be the best option.

A fibreglass jacket was made for the mould, and each piece was removed separately ready for casting. The foundry produced a cast from each piece of the mould and the pieces were then stitched together by lead burning. A stainless-steel armature was built into each lion as the construction progressed, and all joints were fully lead burned and the surface worked back to match the original. The replica leads were finally treated with casein-based paints, which will slowly wear off to be replaced by a natural patina. The replica lions were then securely installed in Stanley Park in Blackpool, on reproduction stone bases.

The east lion, with its left paw raised on a sphere, at Stowe today.

Splendour Captured in Stone

TREVOR PROUDFOOT

Hercules and Antaeus by Peter Scheemakers, copied by Cliveden Conservation, August 2017.

The desired effect: statuary in the South Portico, 1921.

One of the more striking aspects of the restoration of Stowe has been the reinstatement of its statuary.

Following the great sales of 1848 and 1921 the statuary of Stowe – the more portable of the decorative arts – was dispersed throughout Britain and even abroad. Statuary played an important part in the Stowe landscape, adorning not only the temples and monuments in the grounds but also key and prominent positions within and without the mansion. Stowe without sculpture had empty temples, niches without purpose, arenas and hollows without meaning, and vistas without focus. Indeed, even Lord Cobham's pillar was without Lord Cobham, although it was not a sale that removed his huge monumental likeness but a more cataclysmic event in 1951, which is explained below.

His replacement, like all the work in restoring the buildings and landscape of Stowe, has been researched meticulously so that it is hard to detect that this sculpture, now returned, had ever been missing.

The replication of the statuary at Stowe had its beginning in the gift of the landscape garden to the National Trust (NT) in 1989. The latest project will be the completion of the restoration of the south steps and loggia by the return of copies of the four figures (now residing at Easton Neston, Northamptonshire) to their niches, and from St Paul's Walden Bury, Hertfordshire, where they have been since the sale of 1848, the two wrestling groups of Hercules and Antaeus and Hercules and Cacus (also known as Samson slaying the Philistines).

The project of restoring statuary to Stowe started modestly. In 1990, while plans were underway to record the temples and monuments in the landscape, the NT Statuary Workshop at Cliveden, of which I was the manager, was commissioned to undertake a pilot scheme of repair for the State Music Room fireplace: a chimney piece that had lost decoration from the mantle frieze of ox skull bucrania, pendants of canon barrel and gilded brass wire.

The setting of the task to repair this most prominent of chimney pieces, although a relatively small request, had much larger implications. If this job was undertaken well and the chimney piece suitably and impressively restored, then a persuasive case could be more easily put forward for making an early start on renovating other decoration in the wider landscape of the temples and buildings of the estate. The techniques used for replicating lost motifs on the chimney piece frieze, although minor in comparison to reproducing statuary upon pedestals in the temples, were surprisingly similar.

Using the catalogues of the two great sales of 1848 and 1922, we scoured collections and museums for the originals. Most were to be found still in the very places for which they had been purchased. Cottesbrooke in Northamptonshire held the four statues from the Temple of Ancient Virtue, and at Port Lympne, Kent, there were many of the herm statues formerly on the

Fane of Pastoral Poetry in the Stowe gardens and on the north side of the house. Also at Port Lympne was the statue of George II that was missing from his column, and at Bekesbourne, nearby in Kent, two of the ring of seven Saxon deities.

There are three ways of making copies of statues. Traditional means include copy carving and the cheaper method of copy casting. Recently, there has been an increase in the computerised manufacture of statuary. Still a relatively new concept, this method, known as Computer Numerical Control (CNC), is the most expensive and has yet to be used for reproducing statuary at Stowe.

Copy casting has been the most common means of making statuary for the Stowe buildings and landscape. Replica casts are created using moulds of silicone to take impressions of surviving statuary and decoration, and in those moulds copies are produced from mortars of cements and aggregates to replicate the stone.

The mix known as 'artificial stone' is primarily for external display. Statuary cast from artificial stone has a long history, from the Greeks and Romans to the present day. Into a statue mould are placed mortars of aggregate and a cement or lime binder with metal armature reinforcement. Unlike plaster casts the cast is not hollow, but solid. This method is favoured at archaeological sites where copies of originals now on display in museums for their protection are set out in the buildings and landscapes. This 'honest' reproduction of originals can be seen worldwide.

The majority of the statues now in the gardens at Stowe were made by the casting method, with mixes designed at Cliveden Conservation initially with the help of scientist David Speer, formerly of the Cement and Concrete Research Establishment at Slough. The replica casts of the statues in the Temple of Ancient Virtue and six of the seven Saxon deities, all by Peter Scheemakers, were made with a Portland stone artificial stone mix.

There are three parts to the process of making replica casts: mould making, casting itself, and finishing or fettling the completed article.

Removing an original statue for copying.

Mould making
Using the original statue as a model by the application of an elastic material, such as vinyl or silicone, an accurate impression is made. To ensure that the flexible mould is held in the correct overall shape, it is reinforced by a hard case of plaster or fibreglass, which is applied over it.

Replica manufacture
For centuries various formulas have been used for making artificial stone statuary and decoration. A durable mortar of different aggregates to give colour and texture of stone is bound with a mineral cement such as hydraulic lime or the more modern Ordinary Portland Cement (OPC). On curing, the mortar will take the form of the mould into which it has been poured. An internal armature prevents large-scale shrinkage as the mortar cures. Surface shrinkage is minimised by the careful choice of aggregate size and by controlling the amount of water in the mix: too much and the mortar will crack; too little and it will fail to set strongly.

Finishing and fettling
Once the statue is released from the mould, the latter is transported to a place where the copy is made. The sculpture can be reproduced in plaster for internal display, or in artificial stone for outside.

Copy carving is a traditional means of replication, by which the experienced sculptor carves stone blocks. An example of this method is the statue of Lord Cobham situated in the garden at Stowe.

Only the head and the right hand of the posthumous sculpture of Lord Cobham created by Scheemakers in 1751 survived the lightning strike of 1951. The original, like the majority of statuary at Stowe and many other country houses, was carved in Portland limestone, a weather-resistant white stone taken from the lower bed of the quarry. It is a 'freestone', without disfiguring sedimentary-bed lines.

In 1999 it was the turn of Lord Cobham's monument to be repaired and his statue returned to the 23-metre-tall commemorative pillar. Carved from one giant block of Portland stone, he stands at over 2.4 metres, looking out over his Arcadian estate. Cobham is proudly dressed as a Roman general; there is a distinctive Scheemakers' flair to the pose, his right hand holding his cloak and his left on his hip. Although he was to be viewed from a distance and at great height, Scheemakers included much detail, such as the pleats of his skirt festooned with small cameo mask heads.

To carve a replica historic statue requires an understanding of the style of the original sculptor. However, of the Cobham statue only one photograph of any value still existed, taken from some distance at the beginning of the nineteenth century.

A test was set that would show a sculptor's understanding of Scheemakers' distinctive 'classical' style. Taking a surviving fragment from the Cobham sculpture – his right hand with the fingers lost – a number of sculptors were invited to model and carve the hand with the fingers returned. It was a good test, as fingers are not only expressive and indicative of the personality that the sculptor wished to portray, but are also evocative of the style of the period.

A chance reading of an article on Scheemakers by Ingrid Roscoe gave us a great advantage. It is accompanied by a photograph of a similar portrait sculpture, the monument in the church of St Leonard

left to right The mould for Hercules and Antaeus, internal armatures and the statue as it emerges.

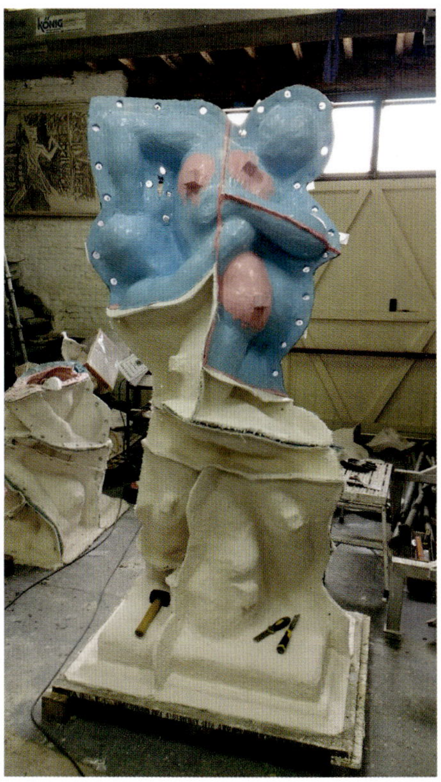

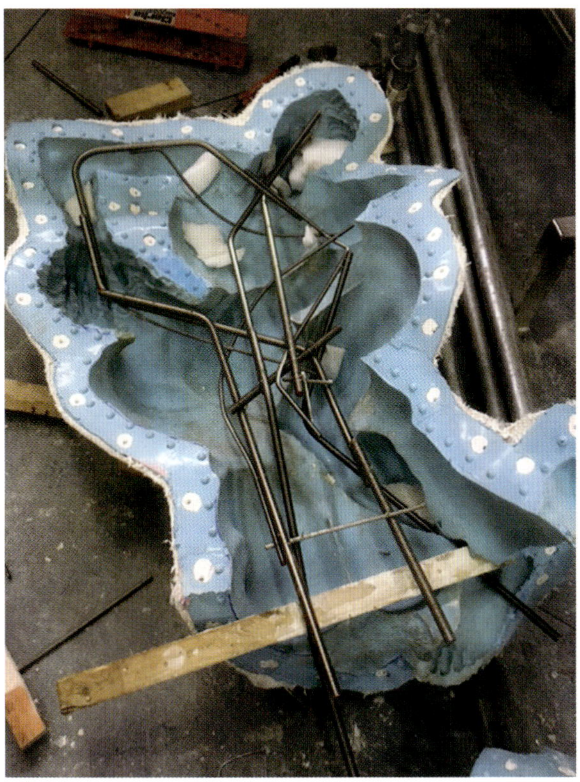

at Old Warden, Bedfordshire, to Sir Samuel Ongley, a contemporary of Lord Cobham and in a similar pose and clothing. Sir Samuel's right hand provided a historical reference for modelling Lord Cobham's hand correctly: the right hand points downwards holding a fold of his cloak, which is compelling evidence that the missing finger was an elegant outstretched index finger and the other fingers are curled in clutching the cloak.

To carve a large lifelike sculpture requires a systematic approach, which starts with a preliminary maquette that serves as a sketch for approval. The pose, proportion and general appearance need to be convincing before moving onto making a full-scale model, from which measurements are taken to create the final carving.

Manually carving a figure such as that of Lord Cobham, including the approval stage of the maquette, can take as long as 20 weeks, which is time enough for the small-scale and full-size clay models to shrink. This can be avoided by using durable materials: the maquette is modelled in wax and the large-scale clay version is cast in plaster.

Measurements may be transferred from the plaster to the stone in a variety of ways, from a simple ruler and a pair of dividers to the more sophisticated pointing machine, a frame with a reticulated arm that effectively holds a point in space. The frame is big enough to surround the full-scale model, and once a point or measurement is taken from the model it is held in space on the end of the reticulated arm, and transferred with the frame. The frame itself is moved across from the model to the stone, and the point measurement is carried within it. The impression of the drill that ensured the point was fixed in the stone often remains even after the final polishing of the statue. Telltale marks of such points or guides are visible on many eighteenth- and nineteenth-century statues, especially those made from marble.

Carving statuary is not a simple mechanical process of stone removal. The art lies in the model. As the figure of Lord Cobham is so tall, perfect modelling was required to ensure a convincingly proportioned set of limbs and torso surmounted by a head. The smallest of inaccuracies in the classical-style figure would render the statue odd-looking.

There can be little doubt that the time spent on life drawing to comprehend the formation and proportion of the human form, allied to experience in repair work adding limbs, fingers and noses to broken statues, and finally time working on real classical statues to understand the Greco-Roman tool marks and sculptor's techniques is essential to the success of such prestigious projects.

The finished work: Lord Cobham atop his pillar.

The Discovery of the Baroque Wall Paintings on the East Staircase

RHIANNON CLARRICOATES

As a paintings conservator and architectural paint researcher, the emerging project on the east staircase at Stowe has been nothing short of thrilling.

At present the staircase has a modest appearance, besides the painted ceiling by Francesco Sleter of *c.*1740 and an adjoining ceiling decorated with *trompe-l'oeil* quadratura, which are the only remnants of a once glorious past. Formerly known as the grand staircase, Benton Seeley's eighteenth-century guidebooks of Stowe describe it as being ornamented with ironwork, and featuring three ceiling pieces – 'Justice & Peace', 'Fame & Victory' and 'Plenty & Constancy' – by Sleter, and as having walls adorned with 'warlike pieces'.[1] However, in the volume *Decorative Painting in England 1537–1837*, Edward Croft-Murray describes Sleter's work in the same way, but notes that the decoration to the walls, and the ceiling paintings of 'Justice & Peace' and 'Plenty & Constancy', had been destroyed.[2] The date when these paintings were lost is not clear, but it may have been during the remodelling works of the 1770s by the 3rd Earl Temple, later the Marquess of Buckingham, as after 1798 Seeley's guidebooks no longer refer to them.

The ceiling ('Fame and Victory') over the east staircase before (*left*) and after (*right*) restoration.

After the completion of a programme of conservation works to the Sleter ceiling – in itself a fantastic project – I carried out some initial investigations into the cornice. The first indication that there might be painterly decoration to the cornice frieze was unearthed in July 2016, when raised outlines of foliate designs were seen in raking light. Authorisation was given to expose a small section of the design through careful removal of the overpaint, and a foliate scroll was uncovered, which bore a striking resemblence to the foliate motifs seen on the ceiling above the upper landing. This exciting discovery not only suggested that the original eighteenth-century wall paintings had survived, but also strengthened the connection between the two ceilings, which currently have a disparate relationship.

Further to this discovery, my team and I were commissioned to undertake a more robust phase of investigation, to establish the extent of the painted decoration and its likely composition. Using a raking light, the walls were carefully examined and the composition marked out where visible. Faint outlines were evident across the walls from skirting level up to cornice height, from the upper landing, down through the staircase and terminating at the pilaster at the foot of the stairs, suggesting the presence of a series of niches, cartouches, overdoor panels, architectural pediments and ashlar blockwork. Interestingly, the composition of wall paintings being intersected by the doors suggests that the door openings on the half landing of the stairs and that leading to the boys' dormitories were later additions.

The texture of the wall plaster made it very difficult to interpret some passages, and it was agreed that several small areas should be uncovered to confirm the presence of significant decoration to the walls of the upper landing, staircase and East Corridor. Following tests, a two-stage mechanical process using scalpels enabled the painstaking removal of the layers

A foliate design exposed in the cornice frieze.

of overpaint to reveal the primary scheme of grisaille, *trompe-l'oeil* paintings. The first tantalising find was some architectural detailing from a niche on the south wall of the upper landing, followed by a pole shaft on the south wall of the staircase, then a section of gilded frame on the north wall of the staircase and, perhaps most exciting of all, a face within a niche on the north wall of the upper landing.

With the discovery of the large expanse of seemingly near-complete wall paintings, we were commissioned to carry out a feasibility study. This began with a more in-depth analysis of the subsequent finishes to the walls, to establish whether they were of any significance in themselves, which would be vital if the wall paintings were to be uncovered. Happily, all later decorative schemes were found to be plain with the exception of the second scheme, which was a pale stone colour with thin white banding. Further investigation of the secondary scheme found a total of four horizontal lines, the full width of the north wall of the upper landing, spaced approximately 48 centimetres apart. These horizontal lines may have been intended to imitate ashlar blockwork and may possibly have been applied following the insertion of the new doorway, which disturbed the original composition of the walls. It is currently felt that sufficient information has been gathered about the secondary scheme. Although not completely plain, it is repetitive in nature and deemed to be of considerably less significance than the primary scheme beneath, and its removal could be considered if the sequence of wall paintings were to be exposed.

In an attempt to appraise better the significance and condition of the wall paintings and to assess the feasibility of uncovering them on a wider scale, we were commissioned to expose a section of 1 square metre in the area where the figure was partially uncovered in the previous phase of testing. The condition of the paintings beneath was generally good, with very little evidence of abrasion, dirt or past intervention. However, two large diagonal cracks were also revealed, which were not apparent previously, as they had been repeatedly filled and scraped back prior to each subsequent scheme of redecoration, masking

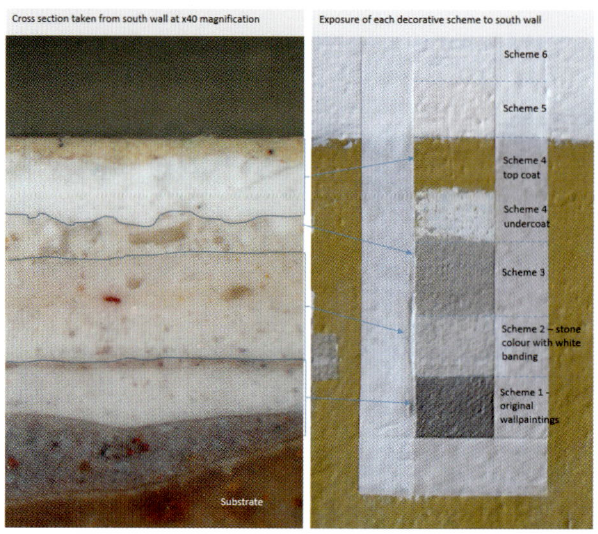

A magnified cross section of paint layers taken from the south wall of the upper landing (*left*) and the exposed layers (*right*).

A revealed section of architectural
detailing from a niche in the
south wall of the upper landing.

left A comparison of the figure of Hope at St Lawrence's Church, Little Stanmore, London (*left*) with that of Minerva found on the north wall of the upper landing at Stowe (*right*).

below left St Lawrence's Church, with the grisaille wall paintings by Francesco Sleter, *c.*1736.

the true condition beneath. The figure within the niche is carrying a shield on her left arm, is wearing a helmet, and may be holding a long spear or staff in her right hand, suggesting that she may be a depiction of Minerva or Athena, and may be one of the 'warlike pieces' Seeley described adorning the walls.

The discovery of this scheme of wall paintings really helps to re-establish the elevated significance of this space and also increases our understanding of how the two spaces connect. There are other examples of Francesco Sleter's work where he has used a comparable approach, most notably St Lawrence's Church, Little Stanmore, London. There, the grisaille wall paintings, dating from *c.*1736, depict reliefs of the evangelists and statues of the cardinal virtues, in contrast to the richly painted ceiling by Louis Laguerre. The resemblance between the two schemes is striking, particularly the niches and modelling of the depiction of Hope at Little Stanmore and the figure of Minerva at Stowe. Using this parallel, one might also speculate that the historic appearance of the ceiling above the upper landing may have been similar to the ceiling of the Chandos Mausoleum at St Lawrence's, which comprises a *trompe-l'oeil* dome surrounded by painted quadratura. Equally, the central oculus at Stowe may have been filled with one of the missing allegorical paintings.

Having found the Baroque wall paintings, a decision must be made about how to proceed. Uncovering might be considered as this is a significant find that brings greater comprehension and coherence to the space. The paintings appear to be in excellent condition and near complete, and the overpaint can be removed safely from the wall paintings on the upper landing, with no obvious signs of damage. There is also a great deal of potential for research, and study of the scheme would contribute to the body of knowledge about the artist and decorative finishes in Britain at that time. With the greater historic, artistic and aesthetic value placed on figurative wall paintings, such research would be likely to safeguard the fabric in the long term and may help to secure funding. However, while it is extremely tempting to reveal the paintings, some constraint must be exercised as there is a wider programme of conservation at Stowe to consider. The discovery increases our understanding of Stowe, yet poses further questions as to the full extent of the scheme of paintings and whether or not they can be located in the west staircase.

My field of work is fascinating, but the project in the east staircase has been particularly enthralling. It has been an honour to convey the secrets held within the walls of Stowe and so rewarding to see the fruits of our labour stimulating new research and discussions among those who know the building intimately.

A conservator at work.

Chapter Four
Stowe Architecture since 2000

ANTHONY WALLERSTEINER

Stowe House remains central to the whole estate.

Stowe presents a uniquely complex challenge as the conservation imperative of restoring the mansion and gardens to the eighteenth-century grandeur of the Temple-Grenville family is balanced against the ever-changing demands of running a successful and dynamic twenty-first-century boarding school that now educates around 800 girls and boys.

Stowe School gifted the gardens to the National Trust (NT) in 1989 so that this palimpsest of landscape gardening history could be enjoyed 'for ever, for everyone'.[1] This was followed by the establishment of the Stowe House Preservation Trust (SHPT) in 1997 to preserve and protect the ducal palace 'for the benefit of the public and the nation'.[2] Since then, the School, SHPT and NT have worked together harmoniously for the good of Stowe. Not only has the mansion been restored so that it can now be fully appreciated as one of the most finely realised neoclassical houses in Europe, set amid the sublime beauty of the landscape garden, but the School has also embarked on ambitious plans to improve its facilities. The departments of music, art, drama and sport, as well as boarding houses, have all benefited from recent infrastructure investment.

Stowe is now treated as a 'gesamtkunstwerk', a project to be considered as a whole, with each constituent consulted on every detail through committees such as the Stowe Advisory Panel, the Partners' Working Group and the Partners' Policy Forum. Together, they ensure that overarching historic conservation and aesthetic principles are applied throughout the site.

Three key documents have informed the restoration programme and the siting and design of new buildings. The Stowe Framework Conservation Plan, originally drawn up by Inskip and Jenkins in 1999 and revised and updated by Dr Sarah Rutherford in 2012, provides essential conservation and planning guidelines for the partnership of the School, SHPT and NT.[3] The second document, drawn up by Rick Mather Architects in 2001 and revised in 2007, is the Stowe School Master Plan, which brings order and coherence to the unruly mix of residential, academic and administrative buildings to the west of the main mansion, formerly Lady Temple's Spinney, a wooded pleasure garden criss-crossed by irregular winding paths that formed an Arcadian backdrop to the Temple of Bacchus.[4] The final document is Towards 2023, the School Development Plan, which sets out the key academic, pastoral and co-curricular targets to be achieved by the time the School reaches its centenary.[5]

An early example of the serendipitous interplay between conservation principles and School development proposals came in 2005 when the School governors were persuaded to embrace full gender equality by allowing girls to enrol from the age of 13 (since 1974 girls were limited to joining in the Sixth Form only). It was decided that the pupil roll should rise to 780 to accommodate the expansion while delivering a welcome and much-needed fillip to the school revenues and academic results.

The governors commissioned Rick Mather Architects to design Queen's and Stanhope, two boarding houses each accommodating 72 girls.[6] A site immediately to the west of Sir Robert Lorimer's Chapel was selected, requiring the demolition of an unprepossessing Clough Williams-Ellis building, Wisteria Cottage, which had most recently been used as an annexe for Sixth Form girls. During planning consultation, the location and orientation of Queen's and Stanhope were adjusted to allow the recovery of a lost avenue, Bridgeman Walk, running between Sir Robert Lorimer's Chapel and the Roxburgh Theatre and culminating at the Temple of Bacchus, a building that had been demolished in 1926 and replaced by the Chapel, which can accommodate 800 Stoics at worship.

The new four-storey building comprises en-suite single, double and quad study bedrooms with staff accommodation on the ground floor and upper levels. The long curved block of Queen's and Stanhope stretches more or less along a north-west axis towards Home Park and has been designed carefully not to compete with Lorimer's imposing Chapel. The sinuous line of the girls' boarding houses is accentuated by a projecting zinc cornice and the mass effect is further reduced by a 3-metre drop in level along its elevation.

Shared facilities include common rooms on each floor with expansive glass panels opening up views to the Chapel and the Western Garden. Each house has its own House Room on the ground floor, with views through to communal gardens, tying together internal and external spaces. The study-bedrooms are accessed by flanking cylindrical glass stair towers that stretch up like illuminated columns to define the main entrances. Glass balustrades with steel handrails link one flight of stairs to the next and large windows suffuse corridors and landings with natural light. South-facing rooms have box oriel window seats, which catch the sun and provide long views of the grounds and adjacent Chapel, while vividly coloured

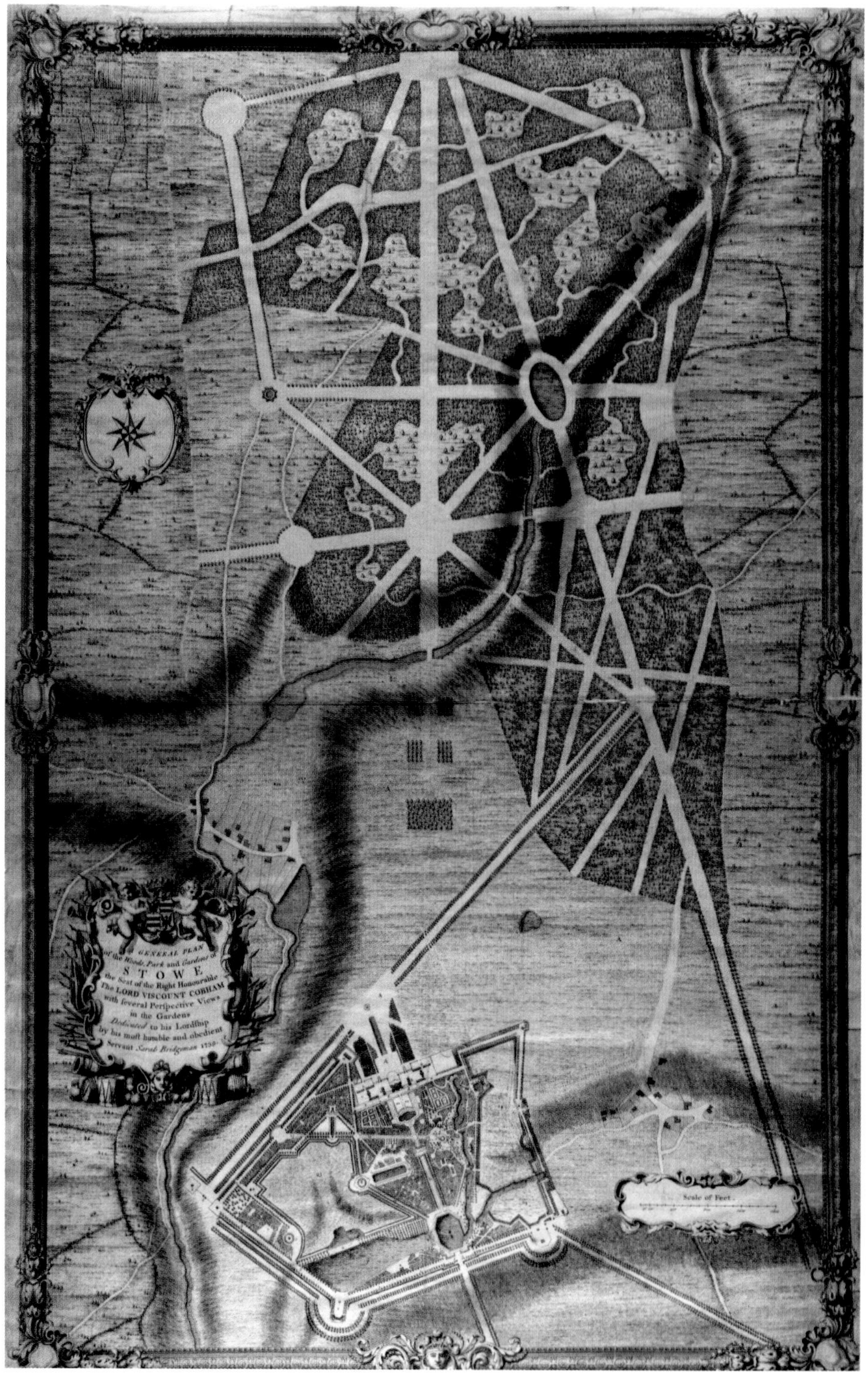

New buildings respect the historical axes and avenues as shown on Charles Bridgeman's survey plan of the estate, published by Sarah Bridgeman in 1739.

The south elevation of Sir Robert Lorimer's imposing Chapel, with Queen's and Stanhope Houses behind.

The interior of Lorimer's Chapel accommodating 800 Stoics at worship.

scatter cushions and teddy bears remind us of the boarding-school context.

A band of Bath stone delineates the ground floor and complements the reconstituted facing stone on Lorimer's Chapel; lime render on the upper floors matches the stucco used on the restored mansion. The building comes into its own on summer evenings when long shadows are cast by the mature trees in the Western Garden and the stone and stucco radiate a warm glow from the setting sun. Queen's House was opened by Her Majesty The Queen on 29 November 2007, while Stanhope was opened on 6 March 2009 by Sir Nicholas Winton, two months before his 100th birthday; Sir Nicholas organised the rescue of 669 mostly Jewish children from Czechoslovakia shortly before the outbreak of the Second World War and has joined the pantheon of distinguished Old Stoic Worthies.

As the number of girls in the School has steadily risen, more pupil accommodation has had to be found. The conversion of Nugent, a Sixth Form girls' house, into a boarding house for girls aged 13 to 18, allowed the governors to even up the girl/boy ratio while making important heritage gains. The buildings that comprise Nugent are attributed to Sir John Vanbrugh and were used previously to provide domestic services for the mansion: a laundry, maids' accommodation and the brewhouse (which became the School's carpentry and maintenance workshop). Rooms in the south-western Nugent block overlooked the visual clutter of Kitchen Court, which the School had designated for storage, a boiler house, oil tanks and general refuse. The creation of a new girls' boarding house gave the School an opportunity to clear the site, create a pleasant outdoor courtyard with a view through to the Chapel, return much of the original fenestration, restore the handsome 1740s' cupola and weathervane, reinstate the lime render and conserve a good example of Vanbrugh's work at Stowe.[7]

After Rick Mather died in April 2013, Rick Mather Architects continued to be involved with Stowe. The wide discrepancy between the standard of girls' and boys' boarding accommodation had not gone unnoticed by pupils, parents or staff. In order to free up more space for boarders, the School governors approved a scheme to convert Cobham House into

opposite Cylindrical glass towers stretch up to define the main entrances of Queen's and Stanhope Houses.

The group of buildings that comprise Nugent House is attributed to Sir John Vanbrugh.

two day houses for girls and boys,[8] named after the School's most illustrious and philanthropic alumni, Lord Cheshire of Woodhall Spa and Sir Nicholas Winton. Cobhamites are the first boys to benefit from new boarding facilities since Bruce House moved out of the mansion in 1984 to purpose-built accommodation. Cobham has been rebuilt in Chapel Court, completing Clough Williams-Ellis's vision of a college quad along the lines of Great Court at Trinity College, Cambridge, where he had studied natural sciences. In Williams-Ellis's 1926 master plan, the south side of Chapel Court was to be enclosed with a classroom block sited just in front of the Ménagerie, thereby designating the Upper Flower Garden as the main east–west axis for the School.[9]

Vanbrugh's Orangery and the south-west façade of the mansion, now Nugent House, provided Williams-Ellis with inspiration for the style and proportions of the classroom buildings in Chapel Court. His master plan made provision for the Chapel, albeit the work of another architect, Lorimer, as a result of a controversial decision by the School governors to reject Williams-Ellis's fussy and suspiciously Catholic design featuring a prominent cupola and clock tower, in favour of Lorimer's more muscular Protestant basilica with its imposing arcade, wagon-vaulted roof, columns recycled from the Temple of Concord and Victory and cedar panelling removed from the former chapel within the mansion. Rick Mather Architects' new boarding house is entirely congruous with its

An architect's impression showing that the relocated Cobham House has been sympathetically designed to match its historic setting, completing the south side of Chapel Court.

A 1926 watercolour by Clough Williams-Ellis showing his conspicuously Catholic design for the Chapel.

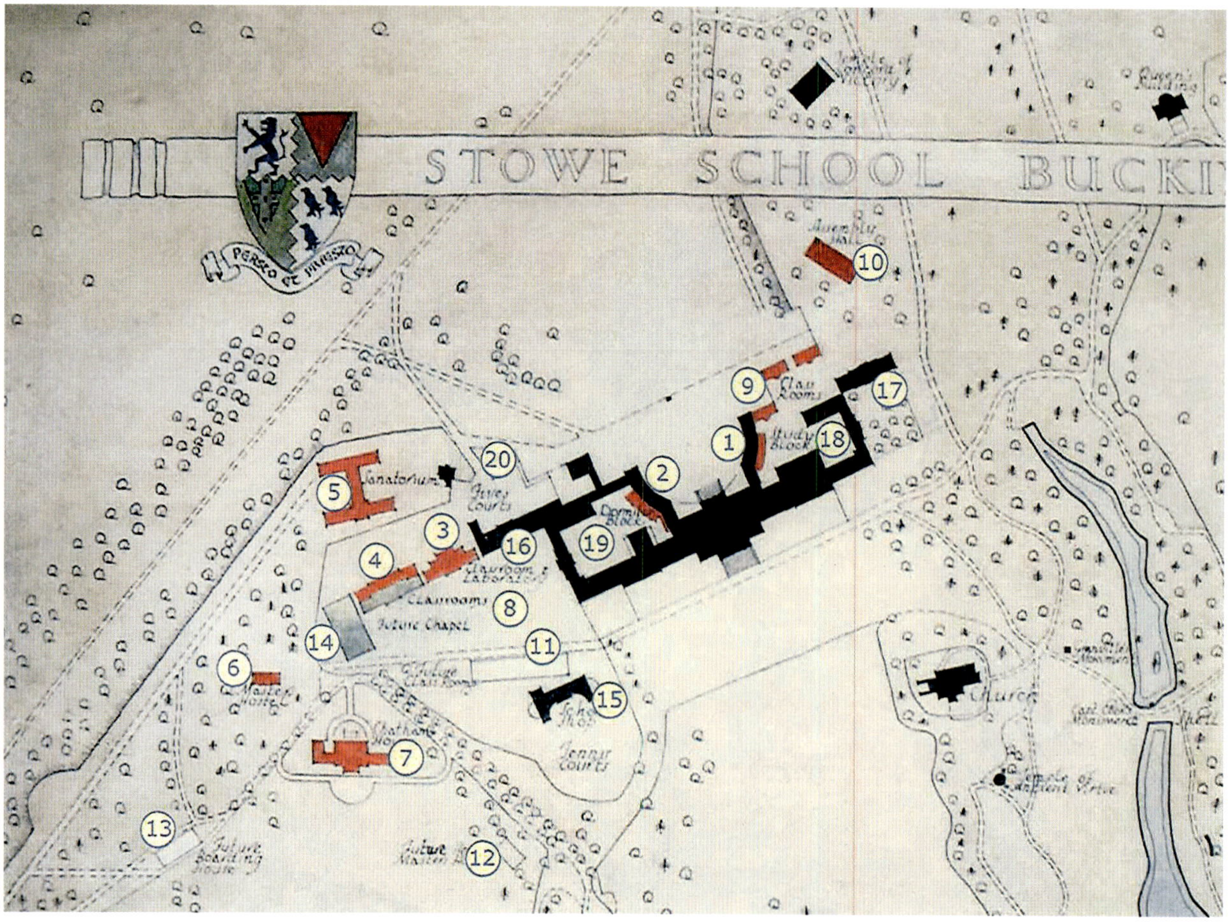

A detail from Clough Williams-Ellis's 1926 master plan.

classical setting and heeds Inskip and Jenkins' exhortation not to commission pastiche buildings that might compete with the masterful designs of Lorimer, Vanbrugh, Giovanni Battista Borra, Robert Adam, Thomas Pitt, Vincenzo Valdrè and Georges-François Blondel.

The relocated Cobham House holds its own as a separate entity and Rick Mather Architects' building blends with the geometry of Chapel Court while clearly belonging to the same family of buildings as Queen's and Stanhope. Just as the earlier boarding house development responds to the adjacency of Lorimer's Chapel, so Cobham is carefully aligned to the height and visual language of the Vanbrugh, Adam and Gibbons classroom buildings. Adjustments have been made to give additional space for the housemaster and his family, a rooftop common room provides stunning views across Chapel Court and a colonnade on the southern elevation pays homage to one of the most iconic features of the North Front. Conservation gains include the reinstatement of Chestnut Avenue (or Gurnet's Walk) as one of the original axes of paths leading to the Temple of Bacchus.

The relocated Cobham House by Rick Mather Architects has been sensitively sized to match the older surrounding buildings.

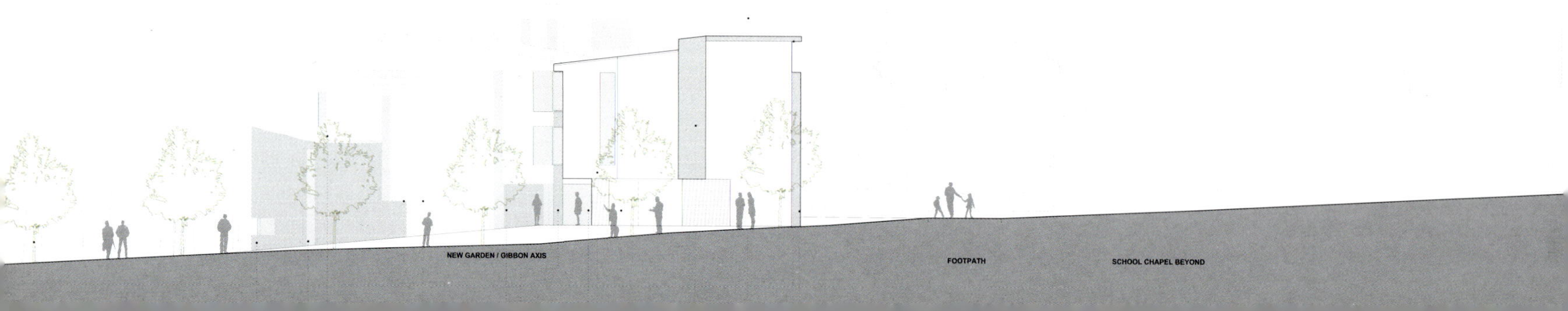

Demand for Sixth Form places remains high and in 2014 the School converted three detached neo-Georgian villas in Home Park, which were built in 1935 for housemasters who left the day-to-day running of their houses to the senior boys, into boarding accommodation for boys and girls. The house was named West to signify its geographical location as well as honouring Gilbert West, a member of the Temple-Grenville family who was also a classicist, poet and politician. In 2017 Rick Mather Architects designed West 5, a building that increased the number of pupils in the house from 30 to 50 and represents arguably the most radical architecture since Lyttelton House was designed by Lyster and Grillet and Harding in 1967. It is characterised by a series of asymmetrically arranged cubist elements, a jazz-like modernist riff on the geometry of the neo-Georgian villas, playfully disrupted by the addition of a cylindrical brick tower. The building walks a tightrope between conceptual and constructivist architecture while blending in and harmonising with earlier styles. The architects show their customary sensitivity to the contextual surroundings of Home Park as a gateway to the Western Garden and further synergy and assonance are achieved by the careful selection of the honey-coloured brick to match the original materials.

One of the central precepts running through the Mather Plan has been to clear away post-war accretions that interfere with the strong geometry of Clough Williams-Ellis's 1926 plan for the academic area. The proliferation of huts and temporary buildings produced a doleful effect as generations of Stoics funnelled through pinch points created by peripheral buildings erected with little or no regard for aesthetic, historic or planning imperatives. New circulation routes were proposed through five zones: the North Approach, the Academic Quarter, the West Wing, Kitchen Court and the South Landscaping.[10]

The North Front and the impressive *cour d'honneur.*

An early gain was the redirection of traffic through a one-way system to reinstate the formal drive to the mansion from the west, thereby honouring the Palladian idea of buildings viewed in their entirety by being approached from an oblique angle. At Stowe, this enables visitors to appreciate the scale and majesty of the impressive *cour d'honneur* added to the North Front in the 1770s. A new pedestrian walkway leads pupils through the Leoni Arch into the academic area where Stoics now find outdoor spaces that complement, enhance and extend existing site geometries. Outdoor rooms include a new courtyard east of the Art School, which is used as a display area for modern sculpture. Another imaginative recasting came with the demolition of religious studies classrooms that had been tacked onto Williams-Ellis's Adam building with little thought to the aesthetic impact on this entry point to the academic area. These rooms have been replaced with raised planting beds that evoke the great parterre on the South Front with its formal planting scheme of boxed yew hedges cut into niches for statuary and urns. A modern statue, *Exuberance*, made in aluminium by Witold Kawalec, a Polish émigré who joined the RAF and fought in the Battle of Britain, welcomes today's Stoics as they go to their lessons. The old squash courts, which were made redundant and replaced by new courts and a fitness centre within the Drayson Sports Centre, have been turned into a popular social area, StoweBucks, furnished with the remnants of a closed-down London nightclub called Crazy Larry's.

A leading Old Stoic benefactor, Lord Sainsbury of Preston Candover, agreed to fund the restoration of the Art School where he had been inspired by the teaching of Robin and Dodie Watts, a Canadian couple who subscribed to avant-garde journals and introduced Stoics to cubism, surrealism and constructivism. The original building, designed by R. Fielding Dodd in 1934, was endowed as a memorial to Old Stoic Pilot Officer G.D. Watson, who was killed in a flying accident in 1932. The rectangular block constructed of brick and finished in stucco is a good example of international modernism. The main studio runs the whole length of the top floor and is lit by a long north-facing window, providing pupils with a superb environment for creative activity. Described unfairly by Brian Stephan as 'not an edifice of any architectural beauty',[11] it has nevertheless produced some of Stowe's finest artists. Unfortunately, decades of neglect, an ugly addition by the Ministry of Defence to accommodate the School's Combined

opposite, top to bottom

Outdoor statuary in the Art School Court.

Exuberance, by Witold Kawalec, welcomes Stoics as they go to their lessons.

The Art School, a rectangular block of brick finished in stucco.

The main studio of the Art School, which runs the length of the top floor, is lit by a north-facing *fenêtre longue*.

Cadet Force (CCF) and a mezzanine floor that destroyed the building's internal unity resulted in the original conception being lost. Rick Mather Architects was appointed to carry out the third phase of the Master Plan. Stitching together new and historic fabric, the architects created three levels of teaching spaces, reinstated the double-height studio, restored the eastern elevation after the demolition of the CCF building, provided top-lit studios, a large gallery and exhibition space on the ground floor leading out to a terrace, and an outdoor classroom for showing contemporary sculpture.[12]

As the School's pupil roll has risen, there has been a commensurate need to improve and extend facilities. An athletics track was opened by Lord Coe in September 2009, named in honour of David Donaldson, an inspirational teacher and coach from 1957 until his retirement in 1973. A new 4G AstroTurf all-weather pitch with additional playing fields vastly improved the School's games provision. An equestrian

The athletics track.

The Equestrian Centre.

centre was built next to Home Farm in 2012 and Captain Mark Phillips designed the cross-country course that opened a year later. The Roxburgh Hall was also completely restored and refurbished. The building dates from the mid-1950s, a time usually considered a low point in the School's evolution as it struggled to recover from the loss of 270 Old Stoics in the Second World War. A period of uncertainty and drift had followed the retirement of the founding headmaster, John Fergusson Roxburgh (known universally as JF), in 1949.

G. Forsyth Lawson, an architect from Banbury, was instructed to draw up a design for a School Hall and Music School at an estimated cost of £16,000 (this rose to £33,000). Seed funding came from a legacy of £5,000 from Dr Huggins, the legendary Director of Music, while further funds were received as donations following the death in 1954 of JF: the Roxburgh Hall, with a neoclassical façade redolent of a provincial theatre, became JF's memorial at Stowe. It is said that a large decommissioned aircraft hangar formed the basis of the construction and, giving some credence to this legend, the Headmaster, Eric Reynolds, wrote in

opposite The exterior and interior of Roxburgh Hall.

1955 that the architect had done a superb job and that 'there is nothing to suggest that the building will look like a hangar in search of an aeroplane'.[13] The keys to the building were handed over to Reynolds at his last Speech Day in 1958.

By the time of the millennium, the Roxburgh Hall was failing to meet the needs of either music or drama. Both departments competed for space in a performance hall that leaked and a lack of rooms meant that it was not unknown for music lessons to take place in the ladies' lavatories (although this did have a resonant acoustic). The glory days when the Beatles performed at Stowe on 4 April 1963, shortly after the release of their first album, *Please Please Me*, were a distant memory.

The Beatles at Stowe in 1963.

The School weighed up the options of demolishing the building and starting afresh or renovating the existing structure. The decision was made in favour of restoration after a visit by the Old Stoic who had masterminded the Beatles concert 50 years earlier. When David Moores stood on the stage of 'the Roxy', where the Fab Four had played their only private concert, and heard that demolition was an option, tears came to his eyes and he resolved to fund the restoration of the Roxburgh Hall.

The work was carried out over three successive summer holidays to allow the building to remain in use for music and drama. The auditorium roof was replaced in the first phase and new tiered seating and the refurbishment of the internal spaces, including the foyer, were programmed for the second year. The final phase involved stripping out the warren of rehearsal and music practice rooms, and creating drama classrooms, a Green Room, improved facilities for visitors and a cleverly designed studio theatre at the back of the stage. The Hall was reopened by Moores to commemorate the 50th anniversary of the Beatles concert.

When the Roxburgh Hall was redesignated the Roxburgh Theatre and handed over entirely to drama, the shortage of music practice rooms and performance spaces had to be addressed. The Queen's Temple had been used as a Music School since 1933 when R. Fielding Dodd enclosed the ground floor arcade for practice rooms. Distance from the main school, the growing demand for music lessons on a bewildering variety of instruments, the increased popularity of music as an academic subject and the emergence of the new discipline of music technology all conspired against the Queen's Temple being considered as a long-term home for Stowe music. In 2008, Berman Guedes Stretton Architects was commissioned to evaluate four possible sites for the new music school.[14] A shortlist of three architects was selected from seven practices that had made a bid for the contract to design the new Music School. Land Use Consultants (LUC) was invited to review the proposals and, in particular, to comment on how the proposals related to the historic landscape in terms of context, views and scale while identifying opportunities for integration and, where necessary, mitigation.[15] Nick Cox Architects, a practice that specialises in the repair and conservation of historic buildings and the design of new buildings in historic contexts, was selected as the architectural practice to deliver this project.

After much discussion, it was agreed that the Music School should be built on a stand-alone site immediately to the west of the Roxburgh Theatre, along the important north-west boundary of the ducal estate known as Nelson's Walk. The most notable feature at this halfway point of Nelson's Walk is Lee's Bastion, the terminus of the Great Cross Walk, an important axis from Charles Bridgeman's garden design leading to the Temple of Ancient Virtue to the east. A second axis is provided by the south-eastern vista towards the Rotunda and onwards to the Octagon Lake. The School's ambition was to establish one of the finest Music Schools in the country, an iconic temple dedicated to Apollo, which would complement and resonate with the neoclassical architecture of the mansion and garden buildings. The User Brief included the following specifications: a recital hall

following pages The Music School: an iconic temple.

with seating for audiences of 250; a recording studio for producing, editing and creating new music; a library to hold one of the largest collections of musical scores of any school in the country; a rock-band room with amplifiers, microphones and recording facilities to allow contemporary rock music to flourish; two classrooms for teaching music and composition as an academic discipline; a percussion room equipped with everything from timpani to tom-toms; a piano room with two Model B Steinways to facilitate teaching through demonstration; 24 practice and teaching rooms; and every piano to be a Steinway or licensed by Steinway. The building would provide a centre for musical excellence, not just for Stoics, but for the wider community given the paucity of venues in Buckingham.

The original design concept presented to the School governors bears a remarkable similarity to the completed building.[16] The fully realised building, the Chung Music School, is an essay in restrained neoclassical modernism and deservedly won a regional RIBA Award in 2014. The architecture makes full use of the contours of the land, which slopes away significantly from the north-west, giving enough height to create an impressive recital hall with views across the Western Garden towards the Rotunda. From the Course, the main approach road between the Boycott Pavilions and the North Front, the building presents a modest and unobtrusive semicircular arrangement of single-storey pavilions that embrace Lee's Bastion, producing an attractive amphitheatre for summer concerts.

Using a radial form centred on the line of the Great Cross Walk, the volume of the building is divided into symmetrical blocks, providing a neat solution to accommodate the different needs of the Music Department: aspects of music-making that require sound-proofing – the recording studio, rock rehearsal room and percussion room – are buried deep in the building where the sound is absorbed by the earth bank, far removed from the pavilions housing strings and woodwind. An important decision was taken by the governors not to economise on materials and the building benefits from extensive use of Bath stone for external walls and the careful selection of internal timber with particular attention given to acoustics.

The central pavilion, the Ugland Auditorium, provides a superb performance space that has already hosted concerts by some of the world's top musicians and orchestras, including a masterclass by Lang Lang and soloists such as Ingrid Jacoby and Philip Fowke. The building was opened by HRH Prince Michael of Kent in May 2015 with a performance of

The Music School's modest and unobtrusive arrangement of single-storey pavilions embraces Lees Bastion.

The interior of the Ugland Auditorium: a superb performance space.

Dmitri Shostakovich's Piano Concerto Number 2 by Stoic soloists accompanied by the Russian National Orchestra. A memorable gala concert followed in the evening when the RNO was conducted by Carlo Ponti with soprano Lesley Garrett as the soloist.

With the completion of new or restored facilities for art, drama and music, the focus now turned to the School's academic provision. The Science Building had been constructed in 1971 when the School roll numbered 600 boys. It reflected Harold Wilson's 'white heat of technology' and was considered 'magnificent' by the Headmaster, R.Q. Drayson, who wrote enthusiastically to the governors that the building provided 'a tremendous stimulus to both masters and boys and is the envy of other schools'.[17] This paean was echoed by Brian Rees, the School's biographer, who wrote in 1989 that the laboratories 'remain one of the best new additions, blending with the North Front approach with a restraint that makes no attempt to distract the visitor's eye'.[18] Most visitors to Stowe would beg to differ with these positive verdicts. While the internal spaces were well designed and benefited from the expert advice of Charlie Macdonald, Head of Science, the original building was austere and unimaginative and situated far too close to the North Front. However, the School roll now stands at nearly 800 pupils and record numbers choose to study the whole spectrum of natural sciences: physics, chemistry and biology. The building was bursting at the seams and unable to cope with the demands of the modern curriculum.

Squires and Brown won the competition to redesign and extend the Science Building, producing a forward-looking and innovative design for six new

The science building before refurbishment: the building had not stood well the test of time.

The refurbished Worsley Science Centre with its imposing glass-fronted entrance and Hamish McKie's Andalusian stallion statue.

SCIENCE CENTRE

laboratories, two for each of the three core sciences. The Sixth Form Study Centre, with its view across to the North Front, has already established itself as a focal point for academic enrichment as well as being home to the biomedical and quantum societies. A lecture theatre lies at the heart of the building and there are ample prep rooms and ancillary facilities. The project was undertaken in four phases, which allowed teaching to take place with minimum disruption (many Stoics professed that they preferred being taught in the temporary portacabin classrooms than the old laboratories). The orientation of the building has been changed with pupil access into a light and spacious atrium through an imposing glass-fronted entrance on the south. The expansion has been made possible by bringing the height of the building up to two storeys while maintaining the original footprint. Facing stone and render replace asbestos panels and industrial bricks with double glazing and new window frames reducing heat loss in winter. The building was opened on 24 January 2017 and named the Worsley Science Centre to honour the distinguished Old Stoic polar explorer and soldier, Lt Col. Henry Worsley, who lost his life exactly one year earlier while attempting a record-breaking solo crossing of the Antarctic.

And what of the future? There is a recognition that the School needs to evolve and adapt if it is to compete effectively and maintain its status as a leading independent school. The main partners working at Stowe – the School, SHPT and NT – have demonstrated that the principles of heritage conservation can be reconciled with the business imperatives of a school that requires modern educational facilities and comfortable boarding houses to attract customers. The partnership has also shown that it is possible to showcase contemporary architecture that embraces modernist designs and the freedom offered by new materials while remaining sensitive to the historic context of the eighteenth-century mansion and the 300 hectares of landscaped gardens and park.

From Stowe House at the eastern extremity of the School site (*top*), educational and boarding facilities have developed to the west, where the asymmetrically arranged cubist elements of West House bring a modernist twist within the historic environment.

GEORGIUS I
REX
MDCCXXVII

Notes

The equestrian statue of King George I on the North Front is a reminder of Viscount Cobham's loyalty to the House of Hanover.

CHAPTER 1: JEREMY MUSSON, PAGES 12–29

1. McCarthy May 1973, pp. 267–98, noted how Stowe had been omitted from major architectural histories of British architecture; Clarke 1990, Bevington 2002a, and various papers published as *Templa Quam Dilecta*. I am especially indebted to Michael Bevington's scholarship, and his study of the complex building history of the mansion house.

2. https://www.stowe.co.uk/house (accessed 19 March 2017).

3. https://www.nationaltrust.org.uk/stowe/features/the-garden-at-stowe (accessed 19 March 2017).

4. Bevington 2002a, p. 9.

5. Beckett 1994, p. 49.

6. Phibbs 2016, p. 41.

7. Robinson 1990, p. 14; Beckett 1994, pp. 116–18, and plate 6, facing p. 116; pp. 120–21 discusses his patronage of Soane at Wotton.

8. Beckett 1994, p. 3; this is a valuable account of the economics of the estate and expenditure of the Temples and the Grenvilles.

9. Ibid., p. 2.

10. Bevington 2002a, p. 9.

11. Ibid., p. 65.

12. Beckett 1994, p. 47.

13. Lewis 1974, to George Montagu, vol. 10, p. 313. In another letter Walpole refers to being 'refreshed with rivers of dew and gentle showers from all the trees', vol. 39, p. 127.

14. Ibid., p. 47.

15. Home 1892, pp. 252–53.

16. Ibid., p. 253.

17. Lewis 1941, vol. 9, p. 122. Lewis suggested that 'Albano' is probably a reference to the landscape painter, Francesco Albani or Albano (1578–1660).

18. Robinson 1990, pp. 111 and 144.

19. Clarke 1990, p. 122.

20. The 1747 version was described as 4th edition 'corrected and enlarg'd', sold by 'B. Seeley, Writing-Master Bookseller and Stationer in Buckingham', whereas by 1750 the title had changed again to: *Stow: the gardens of the right honourable the Lord Viscount Cobham. Containing, I. Forty views of the temples and other ornamental buildings in the said gardens; as also two views of the house. II. A description of all the buildings, copies of the inscriptions, and translations of them. III. A dialogue upon the said gardens.*

21. With thanks to Anna McEvoy of Stowe for her assistance in analysing the various editions of the guides to clarify this point.

22. Buckingham: printed and sold by B. Seeley. Sold also by Messrs G.G.J. and J. Robinson, Pater-Noster Row, London; and Mr Hodgkinson, at the New Inn, Stowe, 1788.

23. Hayden 1991, pp. 21–27.

24. Robinson 1990, p. 39.

25. Ibid., p. 12.

26. Pevsner and Williamson 2003, p. 660.

27. Ibid.

28. Matthew Kilburn. 'Temple, Richard, first Viscount Cobham (1675–1749)', *Oxford Dictionary of National Biography* (Oxford, 2004); online edn, October 2005, http://www.oxforddnb.com.ezproxy2.londonlibrary.co.uk/view/article/27119 (accessed 10 March 2017).

29. Plate 7, as illustrated and explained in Bapasola 2009, p. 17; Vanbrugh's contribution is explored more widely on pp. 15–33.

30. Baggs et al. 1990, pp. 460–70; *British History Online*, http://www.british-history.ac.uk/vch/oxon/vol12/pp460-470 (accessed 19 March 2017).

31. Dixon and Hunt 1988, p. 120.

32. Baggs et al. 1990.

33. Webb (1927) 1967, p. 112.

34. Worsley 2004, pp. 52–57.

35. Hart 2008, p. 208.

36. Lewis 1941, letter to George Montagu, vol. 10, p. 314.

37. Bevington 2002a, p. 39; Brindle 2013, pp. 111–51, pp. 133–35.

38. A sketch for the Blenheim ceiling is in the Victoria and Albert Museum, http://collections.vam.ac.uk/item/O190041/design-for-the-ceiling-of-drawing-thornhill-james-sir/ (accessed 22 March 2017).

39. Robinson 1990, p. 14.

40. Bevington 2002a, p. 8.

41. Ibid., p. 275.

42. Sir John Soane's Museum, London: SM Adam Volume 28/56.

43. Dallaway et al. 1827, p. 84.

44. Lewis 1974, vol. 39, p. 436.

45. Stevens-Curl 2011, pp. 30–31, 34–35.

46. Ibid., p. 50.

47. Ibid., pp. 172–73, as published by John Woolfe and James Gandon. *Vitruvius Britannicus*, vol. IV (London, 1767), plates 49–50.

48. Lewis 1941, vol. 39, p. 127.

49. R.W. Davis. 'Grenville, George Nugent-Temple, first marquess of Buckingham (1753–1813)', *Oxford Dictionary of National Biography*, Oxford University Press, 2004; online edn, May 2009, http://www.oxforddnb.com.ezproxy2.londonlibrary.co.uk/view/article/11490 (accessed 10 March 2017).

50. WMF. 'Technical case study: the Dance of the Hours', https://wmf.org.uk/Projects/technical-case-study-the-dance-of-the-hours/ (accessed 19 March 2017).

51. Stevens-Curl 2011, pp. 55–56.

52. Robinson 1990, p. 153.

53. https://founders.archives.gov/documents/Jefferson/01-09-02-0328 (accessed 22 March 2017).

54. Ibid.

55. Ibid.

56. Robinson 1990, p. 111.

57. Weiss and Quilitzsch (eds) 1997, pp. 10–15.

58. Ibid., p. 60.

59. Ibid.

60. Hayden 1991; Roosevelt 1990, pp. 335–49.

61. Raeburn et al. 1995, pp. 243–35.

62. Ibid., p. 234.

63. 'The Journal of Elizabeth George of Dadford', in I. Toplis et al. (eds). *Recollections of Nineteenth-Century Buckinghamshire* (Buckinghamshire Record Society, 1998), pp. 67–122.

64. Morris 2015, p. 29; the decline of the Grenvilles' fortunes and the sale and dispersal of the estate is explained in Beckett 1994, pp. 251–84.

65. Robinson 1990, pp. 161–64.

66. Information from the Chairman of the SHPT, Andrew Fane, March 2017; this policy was framed at the outset of the interior restoration and conservation programme, but with necessary variation where the evidence is too scant or survival of later phases of significance requires a more nuanced approach.

67. Musson 2009, pp. 58–61; Bevington 2002a, pp. 25–27; Morris 2015, pp. 41–48.

CHAPTER 2: MICHAEL BEVINGTON, PAGES 32–67

1. Beckett 1994.

2. Beckett 1993, pp. 187–99.

3. Bevington 1996, pp. 158–66.

4. Clarke 1990.

5. Williams-Ellis 1923–24, vol. 1: pp. 30–33, vol. 2: pp. 57–59, vol. 3: pp. 88–90, vol. 4: pp. 128–29, vol. 5: pp. 174–75; G. Gilling-Lax. *Some Notes on the History of Stowe* (Stowe School Library, unpublished typescript, 1940); Fitz-Gerald 1973, pp. 572–85; Gibbon 1973, pp. 552–57; Gibbon 1977, pp. 31–44; Gibbon with Clarke 1978, p. 93; Bevington 1990; Pevsner and Williamson, with Brandwood 1994, pp. 660–70; Bevington 2002a; Bevington 2004a. Articles in *The Stoic* are available online at: https://www.stowe.co.uk/school/old-stoics/news/publications/os-archive (accessed 23 September 2017).

6. Clarke 1967, pp. 5–11.

7. Reed 1981, pp. 189–203.

8. Harris 1961, pp. 254–55.

9. Morris 1982, p. 54.

10. Ibid.

11. Clarke 1968, p. 65.

12. Gibbon with Clarke 1968, pp. 158–64.

13. Letters Vanbrugh to Jacob Tonson, 1 July 1719, and 12 August 1725: Webb (1927) 1967, pp. 112 and 167; Whistler 1959, pp. 352–53.

14. Anon. (probably Edward Southwell). 'Account of my Journey begun 6 Aug 1724', Yorkshire Archaeological Society, MS 328, ff.5–6 (printed in Clarke 1990, pp. 18–19).

15. Garden plan no. 8 (fig. 15 in Clarke 1968, p. 75); Rawcliffe 1979, pp. 303–5.

16. 'We shall shortly have a graving of it': John Viscount Perceval, Letter to Daniel Dering, 14 August 1724 (BL Add. MS 47030, ff.156–59); printed in Clarke 1990, p. 15.

17. Bird's-eye drawing of Stowe, attr. C. Bridgeman, Gough Drawings, a.4.fol.46 (Bodleian Library, University of Oxford).

18. Harris 1985, pp. 134–35.

19. On 1 October 1711 Lady Fermanagh from Finmere reported seeing them. In 1724 Lord Perceval saw the 'Art of War' Brussels tapestries, probably of 1706–11: John Viscount Perceval, Letter to Daniel Dering, 14 August 1724, (BL Add. MS 47030, ff.156–59); printed in Clarke 1990, p. 15.

20. J. Loveday. *Diaries* (20 May 1731, 13 June 1735), printed in S. Markham. *John Loveday of Caversham 1711–1789* (Salisbury, 1984), pp. 93, 204–5, reprinted in Clarke 1990, pp. 33–34.

21. J. Milles. 'An account of the journey that Mr Hardness and I took in July 1735', printed in Clarke 1990, pp. 60–61.

22. Bevington 2011.

23. Beckett 1994, p. 37.

24. D. Defoe and S. Richardson. *A Tour thro' the Whole Island of Great Britain*, 3rd ed. (London, 1742), Appendix, pp. 271–87; reprinted in Clarke 1990, p. 83.

25. Temple of Bacchus, S. Serlio. *The Five Books of Architecture* (Eng. trans.: London, 1611), Book III, Ch. IV, Fol. 8; this was also used in Inigo Jones's adaptation for the House of Lords, Westminster.

26. Sophia, Lady Newdigate, Journal (1748, probably 29 July), Warwick RO, CR 1841/7, ff.3–5; reproduced in Clarke 1990, p. 177.

27. H.W. Rodenhausen. *St. Charles Hall* (Lucerne, 2012), pp. 48–59.

28. Sophia, Lady Newdigate, Journal (1748, probably 29 July), Warwick RO, CR 1841/7, ff.3–5; reproduced in Clarke 1990, p. 177.

29. J. Gibbs. 'A Manuscri by Mr Gibbs Memorandums, &c.: A Short Account of Mr James Gibbs Architect And of Several things he built in England &c. after his returne from Italy', MS and typed copy, vol. 26, p. 98, Sir John Soane's Museum; cf. Gibbon 1977, pp. 31–44.

30. Bevington 2006, p. 155, note 10.

31. Anon. 'Anecdotes of Mr Brown, the gardener', *The Morning Post & Daily Advertiser* (30 July 1774), discovered in about 2002, confirming the attribution in: Bevington 1992, pp. 136–63.

32. 'To Mr Flintcroft, a present, six guineas' (17 May 1737, Lord Cobham's account book, ST 161). Gibbon 1977, pp. 31–44.

33. Jemima, Marchioness Grey, Letterbook (5 July 1748), Beds RO, L30/9a/1, ff.164–75; reproduced in Clarke 1990, p. 183.

34. J. de C. *Les Charmes de Stow* (London, 1748), p. 29; reproduced in Clarke 1990, p. 173.

35. Bickham 1750, p. 40.

36. Gadney 1959, pp. 16–18; Whistler 1957, pp. 390–93; Gibbon (with Clarke) 1973, pp. 201–5; O. Zoller. *Der Architect and der Ingenieur: Giovanni Battista Borra (1713–1770)* (Bamberg, 1996); O. Zoller 2001, pp. 217–79.

37. Harris 1964, pp. 173–76.

38. See also: McCarthy 1991, pp. 380–86.

39. Bevington 2006, pp. 140–58; Bevington 2004b, pp. 11–18.

40. 'Palmyra's Temple of Bel destroyed, says UN', BBC News, 1 September 2015.

41. Borra 1753, plate xvi.

42. Gibbon with Clarke July 1975, pp. 145–55; McCarthy May 1973, pp. 267–98.

43. Beckett 1994, p. 84.

44. M. Bevington. *Templa Quam Dilecta, Stowe: XI: the Equestrian Statue of King George I and the North Front* (Stowe, 1989) p. 13; Bevington 2001, pp. 11–17.

45. Bevington 2000, pp. 27–29.

46. M. Bevington. *Templa Quam Dilecta, Stowe: XI: the South Front* (Stowe, 1993), partly reprinted in *The Stoic*, 193 (March 1995), pp. 40–42.

47. Harcourt 1880, vol. 3, p. 123.

48. Tyack and Brindle 1994.

49. Cassidy 2004, pp. 806–14.

50. Bindman 2000, pp. 769–72.

51. Pope-Hennessy 1947, pp. 134–35.

52. Kelly 1992, pp. 97–100.

53. McCarthy April 1973, pp. 221–31.

54. Stuart and Revett 1762, ch.4, plates 10–12 etc.

55. Clarke 1991, pp. 299–319.

56. Gibbon with Clarke December 1975, pp. 221–28.

57. Croft-Murray 1957, pp. 47–53; Gibbon 1965, pp. 238–42; Gibbon 1966, pp. 260–63; Styles 1966, p. 509.

58. Scott 1983, pp. 51–59.

59. McCarthy April 1973, pp. 221–31.

60. Willmert 1993, pp. 26–58.

61. Stroud 1964, pp. 100–1; McCarthy 1985, pp. 129–46.

62. Inskip 2004, pp. 17–24.

63. Bevington 2002b, pp. 26–33.

64. Clarke 1998, p. 114.

65. Christie & Manson, Messrs. *Catalogue of the Contents of Stowe House* (37 days from 15 August 1848), p. viii; *First Supplementary Catalogue* (3 October 1848); *The Remaining Portion of the Supplementary Catalogue* (4–7 October 1848); H.R. Forster (ed.). *The Stowe Sale Catalogue, Priced and Annotated* (London, 1848), p. xliv.

66. Clarke 1973, pp. 8–9.

67. Whitwell 1989), pp. 180–86.

68. Jackson Stops, Messrs. *Stowe, near Buckingham: The Ducal Estate and Contents of the Mansion* (19 days: 4–28 July 1921), 3,955 lots listed.

69. Williams-Ellis 1921, p. 103.

70. Macdonald 1951; Croom-Johnson 1953; N. Annan. *Roxburgh of Stowe: The Life of JF Roxburgh and his Influence in the Public Schools* (London, 1965); Macdonald 1977; Stephan 1998; Rees 2008.

71. Williams-Ellis 1923, pp. 566–76; Powys 1926, pp. 653–60; Williams-Ellis (1924) 1954, pp. 164–65; Williams-Ellis 1971, pp. 139–43; Rawcliffe 1982, pp. 771–77; Haslam 1996, pp. 60–61; Jones 1996, pp. 70–75; Bevington 1997, pp. 12–13; Hughes 2000.

72. Sir L. Weaver. 'Stowe School Chapel', *Country Life*, vol. lxvi, no. 1696 (20 July 1929), 75–77, reprinted in *The Stoic*, iii(6), 19 (July 1929), pp. 245–46.

73. Whitwell 1973, pp. 45–47.

74. Dodd 1934, pp. 175–76; Dodd 1935, pp. 255–57.

75. McInnes 1999, p. 5.

CHAPTER 3: ANNABEL WESTMAN, PAGES 88–90

1. Bevington 2002a, p. 45.

2. Bury 1981, p. 28. I am grateful to Mary Schoeser and Kate Wigley, former archivist at the Warner Textile Archive, for their help in identifying this fabric.

3. 1922 Stowe sale catalogue.

CHAPTER 3: JOHN MADDISON, PAGES 91–94

1. Benton Seeley. *Stowe: a description of the house and gardens of the most noble and puissant prince, George Grenville Nugent Temple, Marquis of Buckingham* (Buckingham, 1820), p. 38.

CHAPTER 3: JOHN DARLINGTON AND NICK MORRIS, PAGES 95–97

1. Michael Reardon, Trustee, SHPT, 4 January 2010.

CHAPTER 3: RHIANNON CLARRICOATES, PAGES 115–19

1. Benton Seeley, *Stowe: A description of the magnificent house and gardens of the Right Honourable George Grenville Nugent Temple, Earl Temple, Viscount and Baron Cobham* (Buckingham, 1780).

2. Croft-Murray 1970.

CHAPTER 4: ANTHONY WALLERSTEINER, PAGES 120–41

1. National Trust marketing motto.

2. Stowe House Preservation Trust: 'the restoration of Stowe House in Buckinghamshire for the benefit of the public and the nation'; Memorandum and Articles of Association incorporated 30 June 1997 and amended by special resolution, 22 September 1999 (charity number 1066272).

3. Dr Sarah Rutherford, Dip. Hort. (Kew), MA, PhD, *Stowe Framework Conservation Plan: The School Estate*, March 2012. This expanded and updated P. Inskip, P. Jenkins, R. Wheeler and K. Felus, *Stowe Framework Conservation Plan: The School Estate*, 4 volumes, 1999.

4. Rick Mather Architects, *Stowe School Master Plan Report*, 2001 and revised 2007.

5. *Towards 2023: Stowe School Development Plan*, 2005, and revised annually.

6. Rick Mather Architects, *Planning Statement and Design Report, Detailed Planning and Conservation Consents Applications Proposed Two Girls' Boarding Houses Stowe School*, June 2005.

7. Network Archaeology, *Nugent House, Stowe, Historic Building Assessment*, Report Number 120468, June 2012.

8. Roberts Limbrick Architects, *Stowe School, Day House and Mansion Master Planning, Feasibility Study*, August 2014.

9. Rick Mather Architects, *New Boys' Boarding House, Stowe School*, 2016, p. 14.

10. Rick Mather Architects, *Stowe School Master Plan Report*, 2001 and revised 2007.

11. Stephan 1998, p. 4.

12. Rick Mather Architects, *The New Art School at Stowe*, 2009. At the time of writing, the School has a notable bronze of figures ascending and descending steps by Lynn Chadwick. The piece is on long-term loan from the Chadwick family.

13. Rees 2008, p. 199.

14. Berman Guedes Stretton, *Stowe School Evaluation of Four Sites for Music Centre*, July 2008.

15. Land Use Consultants, *Proposals for a new Music School, Stowe School, Review of Landscape Context*, November 2010.

16. Nick Cox Architects, *Stowe School, Proposed Music School, Outline Approach to Brief*, May 2010.

17. Rees 2008, p. 267.

18. Ibid.

Chronology

1611

Sir Thomas Temple, a sheep farmer from Warwickshire, purchases a knighthood from King James I.

1677–1683

A new manor house at Stowe is built by Sir Richard Temple, 3rd Baronet. It is designed by William Cleare, who works under Sir Christopher Wren. The house is 13 bays wide and fronted with red brick with quoin details.

1710

Sir Richard Temple's sister, Hester, marries Richard Grenville from nearby Wotton House, thus creating the Temple-Grenville family.

1718

Sir Richard Temple, 4th Baronet, is created 1st Viscount Cobham.

1749

Viscount Cobham dies and the estate passes to his nephew, Richard Temple-Grenville. He gains his title of Earl from his mother.

18th century

Sir John Vanbrugh is believed to have designed the North Front for Viscount Cobham in the early 1720s. Throughout the eighteenth century the house is extensively remodelled and extended.

Earl Temple oversees the redesign of Stowe House as it survives today, commissioning architects including Giovanni Battista Borra, Georges-François Blondel, Robert Adam and Thomas Pitt. The State Drawing Room, Marble Saloon and State Music Room occupy the newly enlarged central pavilion.

The view from the Palladian Bridge.

1774

Lord Temple's nephew and heir, George Grenville, leaves for his Grand Tour around Europe.

1779

Lord Temple dies before the completion of his building project, leaving George Grenville to oversee it.

1796

Richard Grenville, the future 1st Duke, marries Anna Eliza Brydges, the last heiress to the Chandos estate, thus bringing the Chandos name into the title that her husband would take as the 1st Duke of Buckingham and Chandos.

1822

Richard Temple-Grenville is created 1st Duke of Buckingham and Chandos.

1827

The 1st Duke sails around the Mediterranean for three years to avoid his creditors, while buying up classical treasures to bring back to Stowe.

1845

Queen Victoria and Prince Albert visit Stowe, staying for three days. In anticipation of a royal visit, the 2nd Duke spent thousands of pounds preparing the house and grounds, while already in debt to the tune of over £1million.

1848

Poor financial planning and the excess spent on the royal visit lead to the sale of much of the contents of the Stowe estate. Notable lots include the Chandos portrait of William Shakespeare and the State Bed in which the royal visitors had slept. At this point, much of the statuary and the important painting collection are also sold.

1861

Richard, the 3rd Duke, inherits the estate and takes the longest non-repetitive surname in Britain: Temple-Nugent-Brydges-Chandos-Grenville.

1889–1894

The estate is let to the Comte de Paris, claimant to the French throne, after the death of the 3rd Duke.

1914

Richard Morgan-Grenville, Master of Kinloss and heir to the Stowe estate, is killed in Flanders just before Christmas.

1921

The family finances are unable to recover and Stowe is sold to Harry Shaw, a property developer, who intends to present Stowe to the nation.

1922

Shaw lacks the necessary endowment and the government declines his offer. Shaw strips the house of its original fittings and sells the empty estate to the Martyrs Memorial Trust (later Allied Schools Group), which intends to establish a new boarding school.

1923

Clough Williams-Ellis is employed to oversee the renovation of the house and creation of the classrooms, dormitories and bathrooms required for its new use. Stowe School's first Headmaster, J.F. Roxburgh, welcomes the first cohort of 99 boys.

1970

Stowe School opens the gardens and State Rooms to the public.

1989

Stowe School passes the freehold of the extensive gardens and parkland to the National Trust (NT) on a long-term agreement. The NT opens the gardens to the public and has since carried out extensive restoration work to the landscape and surviving monuments. A 125-year renewable lease and under-lease allow the use of the gardens and parkland by NT visitors and Stowe School.

1997

The Stowe House Preservation Trust (SHPT) is founded in order to raise funds for and manage the restoration of the house, including the external fabric and surviving state interiors, and also to take on responsibility for presenting and opening the house to the public.

2002

Stowe House is placed on World Monuments Fund list of the 100 most endangered sites.

2010

Completion of restoration of the most important elevations of Stowe House by the SHPT.

2011–2015

Ongoing restoration of interior spaces by the SHPT: Library and Ante-Library (2010), Egyptian Hall (2011), State Music Room (2012), East Corridor floors (2013) and Blue Room (2014–15).

2013

Restoration of the South Front balustrade, reinstatement of the Medici Lions and the installation of replica copper urns along the balustrade.

2015

The Welcome Centre, Discovery Centre and education facilities are opened by the SHPT in the old servants' hall and wine cellar of Stowe House.

The Temple-Grenville Family

Owners of Stowe are shown in BLUE.

- **PETER TEMPLE**
  Took lease of Stowe 1571 (d.1578)
  m. Millicent, daughter of William Jekyll of Newington, Co. Middlesex
  - **JOHN TEMPLE**
    (1542–1603)
    m. Susan Spencer
    - **SIR THOMAS TEMPLE, MP**
      Cr. Knight 1603
      1st Baronet 1611 (?1566–1637)
      m. Hester Sandys (1569–1656)
      - **SIR PETER TEMPLE**
        2nd Baronet, MP (1592–1653)
        (1) m. Anne Throckmorton (d.1619/20)
        (2) m. Christian Leveson (d.1655)
        - **SIR RICHARD TEMPLE**
          3rd Baronet, MP (1634–97)
          m. Mary Knapp (d.1726)
          - **SIR RICHARD TEMPLE**
            4th Baronet, Cr. Baron Cobham 1714,
            Cr. 1st Viscount Cobham 1718 (1675–1749)
            m. Anne Halsey (d.1760)
          - **MARIA**
            (1683–1763)
            m. Rev. Richard West
          - **HESTER**
            Baroness Cobham
            Viscountess Cobham
            and Countess Temple (1684–1752)
            m. Richard Grenville of Wotton (1677–1727)
            - **RICHARD GRENVILLE**
              2nd Earl Temple, MP (1711–79)
              m. Anna Chamber (1709–77)
            - **GEORGE GRENVILLE**
              Prime Minister (1712–70)
              m. Elizabeth Wyndham (d.1769)
              sister of the 1st Earl of Egremont
              - **GEORGE**
                Cr. 1st Marquess of Buckingham 1784 (1753–1813)
                m. Lady Mary Elizabeth Nugent (1758–1812)
                Baroness Nugent of Carlanstown
                - **RICHARD**
                  2nd Marquess of Buckingham
                  Cr. 1st Duke of Buckingham and Chandos 1822 (1776–1839)
                  m. Lady Anna Eliza Brydges (1779–1835),
                  Baroness Kinloss, heiress of 3rd Duke of Chandos
                  - **RICHARD**
                    2nd Duke of Buckingham and Chandos (1797–1861)
                    m. Lady Mary Campbell (1795–1862)
                    - **RICHARD**
                      3rd Duke of Buckingham and Chandos (1823–89)
                      (1) m. Caroline Harvey (1823–74)
                      (2) m. Alice Anne Montgomery (1847–1931)
                      - **LADY MARY**
                        Baroness Kinloss (1852–1944)
                        m. Major Luis Morgan-Grenville (1860–96)
                        - **RICHARD MORGAN-GRENVILLE**
                          Master of Kinloss (1887–1914)
                          died in action
                        - **REV. LUIS**
                          Sold Stowe 1921 (1889–1944)
                          m. Katherine Jackman (d.1960)
                    - **LADY ANNA ELIZA MARY GRENVILLE**
                      (1820–70)
                      m. William Henry Powell Gore-Langton (1824–73)
                      - **EARLS TEMPLE OF STOWE**
                - **GEORGE GRENVILLE**
                  2nd Baron Nugent
              - **THOMAS GRENVILLE**
                (1755–1846)
              - **WILLIAM WYNDHAM GRENVILLE**
                Cr. 1st Baron Grenville 1790,
                Prime Minister (1759–1834)
            - **JAMES**
              (1715–83)
            - **HENRY**
              (1717–84)
            - **THOMAS**
              Capt RN (1719–47),
              died in action
            - **HESTER**
              1st Baroness Chatham
              (1721–1803)
          - **CHRISTIAN**
            (1680–1748)
    - **SIR JOHN TEMPLE**
      m. Anne Tomlins

opposite The Temple of British Worthies reflects the men and women of action and letters who were admired by the Temple-Grenvilles.

Select Bibliography

The Library.

N. Annan. *Roxburgh of Stowe: The Life of JF Roxburgh and his Influence in the Public Schools* (London, 1965)

A.P. Baggs et al. 'Blenheim: Park from 1705', in Alan Crossley and C.R. Elrington (eds). *A History of the County of Oxford: Volume 12, Wootton Hundred (South) Including Woodstock* (London, 1990), pp. 460–70

J. Bapasola. *The Finest View in England: The Landscape and Gardens at Blenheim Palace* (Blenheim, 2009)

J.V. Beckett. 'The Stowe papers', *Archives*, vol. xx (October 1993), pp. 187–99

J.V. Beckett. *The Rise and Fall of the Grenvilles: Dukes of Buckingham and Chandos, 1710 to 1921* (Manchester and New York, 1994)

M. Bevington. *Templa Quam Dilecta, Stowe: IV: the Equestrian Statue of King George I and the North Front* (Stowe, 1989)

M. Bevington. *Stowe House* (Stowe, 1990)

M. Bevington. 'The development of the classical revival at Stowe', *Architectura*, vol. xxi, no. 2 (1992), pp. 136–63

M. Bevington. *Templa Quam Dilecta, Stowe: XI: the South Front* (Stowe, 1993)

M. Bevington. *Stowe: The Garden and the Park*, 3rd ed. (Stowe, 1996)

M. Bevington. 'Clough-Williams Ellis at Stowe', *The Stoic*, 195 (March 1997), pp. 12–13

M. Bevington. 'The Stowe herms', *The Stoic*, 199 (September 2000), pp. 27–29

M. Bevington. 'Behind the façade (seven stages in the development of the North Front)', *The Stoic*, 200 (September 2001), pp. 11–17

M. Bevington. *Stowe House* (London, 2002a)

M. Bevington. 'Nugent House', *The Stoic*, 201 (September 2002b), pp. 26–33

M. Bevington. *Stowe: The Bibliography: The Landscape Garden, Park, House, Estate and School, Country Life* (Leeds, 2004a)

M. Bevington. 'Stowe's Garter Room: the birthplace of neo-classical architecture in England', *The Stoic*, 203 (June 2004b), pp. 11–18

M. Bevington. 'The Garter Room at Stowe House', *The Georgian Group Journal*, vol. xv (2006), p. 155, note 10

M. Bevington. *Stowe: The People and the Place* (London, 2011)

G. Bickham, *The Beauties of Stowe* (May's building and the New Inn, 1750)

D. Bindman. 'Thomas Banks's "Caractacus before Claudius": new letters to and from Ozias Humphrey', *The Burlington Magazine*, vol. cxlii, no. 1173 (December 2000), pp. 769–72

J.-B. Borra. 'Plan of the temple [of the Sun] and its peristyle', plate xvi, in R. Wood. *The Ruins of Palmyra, otherwise Tedmor, in the Desart* (London, 1753)

S. Brindle. 'Kent the painter', in Susan Weber. *William Kent: Designing Georgian Britain* (London and New Haven, 2013), pp. 111–51, pp. 133–35

H. Bury. *A Choice of Design 1850–1980: Fabrics by Warner & Sons Ltd*, exh. cat. (London, 1981)

B. Cassidy. 'Thomas Pitt and statues for Stowe', *The Burlington Magazine*, vol. clvi, no. 1233 (December 2004), pp. 806–14

G.B. Clarke. 'The history of Stowe: III: the rise of the Temple family', *The Stoic*, 134 (December 1967), pp. 5–11

G.B. Clarke. 'The history of Stowe: IV: Sir Richard Temple's house and gardens', *The Stoic*, 135 (March 1968), pp. 65–80

G.B. Clarke. 'The Ducal gasworks', *The Stoic: A Stowe Miscellany* (1973), pp. 8–9

G.B. Clarke (ed.). *Descriptions* of Lord Cobham's Gardens at *Stowe* 1700–1750 (Aylesbury, 1990)

G.B. Clarke. 'The lady with the squint: an examination of the revolutionary iconography at Stowe', *La Grecia Antica Mito e Simbolo per l'Età della Grande Rivoluzione* (Milan, 1991), pp. 299–319

G.B. Clarke (ed.). 'The journal of Elizabeth George of Dadford', in *Recollections of Nineteenth-century Buckinghamshire* (Aylesbury, 1998), pp. 65–122

E. Croft-Murray. 'Un decorator faentino in Inghilterra: Vicenzo Valdrati o Valdrè (1742–1814)', *Studi Romagnoli* (1957), pp. 47–53

E. Croft-Murray, *Decorative Painting in England 1537–1837, Volume 2: The Eighteenth and Nineteenth Centuries* (London, 1970)

The Hon. Sir R.P. Croom-Johnson. *The Origin of Stowe School* (Ipswich and London, 1953)

J. Dallaway et al. *Anecdotes of Painting* (London, 1827)

J. Dixon Hunt. *The Genius of the Place: The English Landscaped Garden, 1620–1820* (Cambridge, MA, 1988)

R.F. Dodd. 'Walpole House', *The Stoic*, 35 (December 1934), pp. 175–76

R.F. Dodd. 'New work at Stowe School', *Architectural Review* (1935), pp. 255–57

D.J.V. Fitz-Gerald. 'A history of the interior of Stowe', *Apollo*, vol. xcvii, no. 136 (June 1973), pp. 572–85

R.B.J. Gadney. 'Borra's contribution to Stowe', *The Stoic*, 110 (December 1959), pp. 16–18

M.J. Gibbon. 'Valdrè, *The Stoic*, 127 (August 1965), pp. 238–42

M.J. Gibbon. 'A forgotten Italian at Stowe: Vicenzo Valdrè, architect and painter', *Country Life*, vol. cxl (4 August 1966), pp. 260–63

M.J. Gibbon. 'Stowe House, 1680–1779', *Apollo*, vol. xcvii, no. 136 (June 1973), pp. 552–57

M.J. Gibbon. 'Stowe, Buckinghamshire: the house and garden buildings and their designers. A catalogue', *Architectural History*, vol. xx (1977), pp. 31–44

M.J. Gibbon (with G.B. Clarke). 'The history of Stowe: VI: Lord Cobham's house', *The Stoic*, 137 (December 1968), pp. 158–64

M.J. Gibbon (with G.B. Clarke). 'The history of Stowe, XVIII: Earl Temple and Giambattista Borra', *The Stoic*, 150 (March 1973), pp. 201–5

M.J. Gibbon (with G.B. Clarke). 'The history of Stowe, XXII: the rebuilding of the house', *The Stoic*, 155 (July 1975), pp. 145–55

M.J. Gibbon (with G.B. Clarke). 'The history of Stowe, XXIII: Lord Buckingham and the completion of the interior', *The Stoic*, 156 (December 1975), pp. 221–28

M.J. Gibbon (with G.B. Clarke). 'Addenda to Stowe, Buckinghamshire', *Architectural History*, vol. xxi (1978), p. 93

E.W. Harcourt (ed.). *The Harcourt Papers* (Oxford, 1880)

J. Harris. 'Wren's work at Stowe (Correspondence)', *Country Life*, vol. cxxx (3 August 1961), pp. 254–55

J. Harris. 'Blondel at Stowe', *The Connoisseur*, vol. clv (March 1964), pp. 173–76

J. Harris. *The Design of the English Country House 1620–1920* (London, 1985)

V. Hart. *Sir John Vanbrugh: Storyteller in Stone* (London and New Haven, 2008)

R. Haslam. *Clough Williams-Ellis* (London, 1996), pp. 60–61

P. Hayden. 'The Russian Stowe: Benton Seeley's guidebooks as a source of Catherine the Great's park at Tsarskoye Selo', *Garden History*, vol. 19, no. 1 (Spring 1991), pp. 21–27

J. Home (ed.). *The Letters & Journals of Lady Mary Coke*, vol. III (Edinburgh, 1892)

K. Hughes. 'Stowe: "Cherish the past, adorn the present, construct the future" – the adaptation of a great country house to a public school at Stowe by Clough Williams-Ellis' (University of York: unpublished MA thesis, August 2000)

P. Inskip. 'Soane and the Grenvilles', *Apollo*, vol. clix, no. 506 (April 2004), pp. 17–24

J. Jones. *Clough Williams-Ellis, The Architect of Portmeirion* (Bridgend, 1996)

A. Kelly. 'Eleanor Coade at Stowe', *The Georgian Group Journal* (1992), pp. 97–100

W.S. Lewis (ed.). *The Yale Edition of Horace Walpole's Correspondence* (48 vols, New Haven, 1937–1983)

A. Macdonald. *Stowe: House and School* (Ipswich, 1951)

A. Macdonald. *Stowe School: An Illustrated History* (London, 1977)

M.J. McCarthy. 'James Lovell and his sculptures at Stowe', *The Burlington Magazine*, vol. cxv, no. 841 (April 1973), pp. 221–31

M.J. McCarthy. 'The rebuilding of Stowe House, 1770–1777', *Huntington Library Quarterly*, vol. 36, no. 3 (May 1973), pp. 267–98

M.J. McCarthy. 'Soane's 'Saxon' Room at Stowe', *Journal of the Society of Architectural Historians*, vol. xliv (May 1985), pp. 129–46

M.J. McCarthy. 'Thomas Pitt, Piranesi and John Soane: English architects in Italy in the 1770s', *Apollo*, vol. cxxxiv, no. 358 (December 1991), pp. 380–86

C. McInnes. 'The Stowe House Preservation Trust', *The Stoic*, 197 (March 1999), p. 5

C. Morris (ed.). *The Illustrated Journeys of Celia Fiennes* (London, 1982)

N. Morris. *The Essential Stowe House* (London, 2015)

J. Musson. 'A triumphant return: the Marble Saloon, Stowe, Buckinghamshire', *Country Life*, vol. 203, no. 42 (21 October 2009), pp. 58–61

N. Pevsner and E. Williamson. *Buildings of England: Buckinghamshire* (London and New Haven, 2003)

N. Pevsner and E. Williamson, with G. Brandwood. *The Buildings of England: Buckinghamshire* (Harmondsworth, 1994)

J. Phibbs. *Capability Brown: Designing the English Landscape* (New York, 2016)

J. Pope-Hennessy. 'A relief by Veyrier at Stowe', *The Burlington Magazine*, vol. lxxxix, no. 530 (May 1947), pp. 134–35

A.R. Powys. 'Mr Williams-Ellis' new buildings at Stowe', *The Architects' Journal* (28 April 1926), pp. 653–60

M. Raeburn et al. *The Green Frog Service* (London, 1995)

R.C. Rawcliffe. 'Vanbrugh's work at Stowe', *The Stoic*, 163 (July 1979), pp. 303–5

R.C. Rawcliffe. 'An architectural history of Chatham House', *The Stoic*, 170 (December 1982), pp. 771–77

M. Reed. 'Seventeenth-century Stowe', *The Huntington Library Quarterly*, vol. xliv (1981), pp. 189–203

B. Rees. *Stowe: The History of a Public School, 1923–1989* (London, 2008)

J.M. Robinson. *Temples of Delight: Stowe Landscape Gardens* (London, 1990)

P.R. Roosevelt. 'Tatiana's garden: noble sentiments and estate park design in the Romantic era', *Slavic Review*, vol. 49, no. 3 (Autumn 1990), pp. 335–49

J. Scott. 'Another chimney piece by Piranesi', in A. Bettagno (ed.). *Piranesi: Tra Venezia e l'Europa* (Florence, 1983), pp. 51–59

B. Seeley. *Stowe: a description of the magnificent house and gardens of the Right Honourable George Grenville Nugent Temple, Earl Temple, Viscount and Baron Cobham* (Buckingham, 1780)

B. Seeley. *Stowe: a description of the house and gardens of the most noble and puissant prince, George Grenville Nugent Temple, Marquis of Buckingham* (Buckingham, 1820)

B. Stephan. *Stowe: Hearsay and Memory* (Stowe, 1998)

J. Stevens-Curl. *Georgian Architecture in the British Isles, 1714–1830* (Swindon, 2011)

D. Stroud. 'The Gothic Library', *The Stoic*, 124 (August 1964), pp. 100–1

J. Stuart and N. Revett. *The Antiquities of Athens and Other Monuments of Greece* (London, 1762)

D.L. Styles. 'Valdrè painting traced' [letters], *Country Life*, vol. cxl (1 September 1966), p. 509

G. Tyack and S. Brindle. *Blue Guide. Country Houses of England* (London, 1994)

G. Webb (ed.). *The Complete Works of Sir John Vanbrugh*, vol. IV, The Letters, 1927 (reprinted New York, 1967)

T. Weiss and U. Quilitzsch (eds). *For the Friends of Nature and Art: The Garden Kingdom of Prince Franz von Anhalt-Dessau in the Age of Enlightenment* (Ostfildern-Ruit, 1997)

L. Whistler. 'Signor Borra at Stowe', *Country Life*, vol. cxxii (29 August 1957), pp. 390–93

L. Whistler. 'Vanbrugh's work at Stowe House', *Country Life*, vol. cxxv, no. 3240 (19 February 1959), pp. 352–53

S. Whitwell. 'Stowe architecture: the School's contribution', *The Stoic: A Stowe Miscellany* (11 May 1973), pp. 45–47

S. Whitwell. 'Expelled to Stowe: the Comte de Paris in exile', *Country Life*, vol. clxxxii, no. 49 (7 December 1989), pp. 180–86

A. Williams-Ellis. *The Pleasures of Architecture* (London, 1924; 2nd ed. 1954), pp. 164–65

C. Williams-Ellis. 'Stowe, past and future', *The Spectator*, vol. cxxvii (23 July 1921), p. 103

C. Williams-Ellis. 'The conversion of Stowe', *The Architects' Journal* (28 March 1923), pp. 566–76

C. Williams-Ellis. 'The fabric of Stowe: I–V', *The Stoic*, vols 1–5 (July 1923–December 1924), 1: pp. 30–33, 2: pp. 57–59, 3: pp. 88–90, 4: pp. 128–29, 5: pp. 174–75

C. Williams-Ellis. *Architect Errant* (London, 1971), pp. 139–43

T. Willmert. 'Heating methods and their impact on Soane's work: Lincoln's Inn Fields and Dulwich Picture Gallery', *Journal of the Society of Architectural Historians*, vol. LII, no. 1 (March 1993), pp. 26–58

G. Worsley. 'Stowe House', *Country Life* (29 January 2004), pp. 52–57

O. Zoller. *Der Architect and der Ingenieur: Giovanni Battista Borra (1713–1770)* (Bamberg, 1996)

O. Zoller. 'Giovanni Battista Borra disegnatore e architetto nel Levante e in Inghilterra', in G. Dardanello (ed.). *Sperimentare l'architettura, Guarini, Juvarra, Alfieri, Borra e Vittone*, vol. 15 of G. Romano (ed.). *Arte in Piemonte* (Turin, 2001), pp. 217–79

Author Biographies

PATRICK BATY is interested in the decoration of historic buildings. His work covers research, paint analysis, colour and technical advice, and colour surveys. Projects have ranged from King Henry VIII's heraldic beasts, Baroque churches, country houses, wartime RAF stations and London social housing estates to structures such as Tower Bridge and Holborn Viaduct. He also works in the USA. In 2017, Thames & Hudson published his first book, *The Anatomy of Colour*.

MICHAEL BEVINGTON started teaching at Stowe in 1978 and was Head of Classics for 30 years from 1986. Since the 1980s he has researched the history of Stowe's garden and house. His publications include the *Templa Quam Dilecta* series, *Stowe: A Guide to the House* (1990) and *Stowe House* (2002). His work here outlines his current thinking on the development of Stowe House.

RHIANNON CLARRICOATES ACR MA BA (Hons) is an accredited paintings conservator and architectural paint researcher who has been employed for the past 13 years at Hirst Conservation. Since 2014 she has worked as an associate lecturer for the conservation department at the School of History and Heritage, University of Lincoln. She is a trainee assessor for the Conservation and Collections Care Technician's diploma (V&A and Institute of Conservation). Rhiannon acted as secretary of the Icon Paintings Group for ten years, organising a number of conferences and co-editing three sets of published post-prints.

JOHN DARLINGTON was appointed Executive Director of World Monuments Fund Britain in March 2015. Since then he has been involved in a diverse range of conservation projects, including establishing a conservation stone-masonry training school for Syrian refugees in Jordan and helping to guide archaeologists in Iraq as they tackle the challenge of post-conflict conservation. John's ongoing work for WMF at Stowe sits alongside initiatives to breathe new life into other endangered buildings. An archaeologist by background, John has also worked as Regional Director for the National Trust and at various local authorities across the UK.

ANDREW FANE read Law at Cambridge before qualifying as a Chartered Accountant and worked for 25 years in the City. He changed direction in the 1990s and joined the Board of Great Ormond Street Hospital, where he served as Non-Executive Director for 20 years. In 1995 he joined the Commission of English Heritage where he chaired the London Committee and the Historic Buildings Council. He was Chairman of the Foundling Museum, and is Chairman of Chiswick House and Gardens Trust. He is actively involved in Emmanuel College, Cambridge, where he is an Honorary Fellow and President of the Emmanuel Society.

RUPERT HARRIS established his practice in 1982, and his studio has since built an international reputation for the conservation of sculpture, particularly metals. He advises national institutions including the National Trust and Historic England. Rupert is an elected Fellow of the Royal Society of Arts and holds a PACR (Professional Accreditation of Conservator-Restorers) awarded by the Institute of Conservation.

JANE KENNEDY is a partner at Purcell and has been architect at Stowe House since 1999. She has held personal appointments at Ely, Christ Church and Newcastle cathedrals and was architect for the conversion in Eire of the Ballyfin Demesne to a country-house hotel. She is currently a trustee of Historic Royal Palaces.

JOHN MADDISON FSA is an artist and architectural historian. A former Architectural Adviser to the Victorian Society and Historic Buildings Representative to the National Trust, he now undertakes decorative and furnishing projects in cathedrals, parish churches and country houses, prepares conservation management plans, and paints landscape and still life.

ANNA MCEVOY has worked at Stowe for over ten years having previously run Heritage Lottery Projects at Chiltern Open Air Museum, created an education programme at Bradwell Abbey, Milton Keynes, and taught A-Level History. Her current involvement in the research and restoration of the Stowe House State Rooms enables her to get back to her roots in building archaeology and investigation.

JEREMY MUSSON is an architectural historian, lecturer and author; architectural editor of *Country Life* magazine (1998–2007); and a former National Trust assistant regional curator (1993–95). Jeremy also presented BBC2's TV series *The Curious House Guest*. He is a trustee of the Stowe House Preservation Trust and a member of its Interiors Working Group; he is also a trustee of the Country Houses Foundation.

Acknowledgements

TREVOR PROUDFOOT trained as a stonemason in London in the 1970s. Following conservation of the notable monument The Bristol Cross at Stourhead, he set up the National Trust Statuary Workshop at Cliveden in 1982. In 1991 the workshop became Cliveden Conservation, a private company retaining strong links with the National Trust while undertaking work for others. Cliveden has been responsible for the repair of the carved stonework on the north and south façades of Stowe as well as the repair of the decorative ceilings of the Marble Saloon and the Library.

DR ANTHONY WALLERSTEINER has been Headmaster of Stowe since 2003. He was educated at King's Canterbury, won an open scholarship to Trinity College Cambridge and awarded a Ph.D. at Kent University. He has taught at St Paul's, Sherborne and Tonbridge, and served as a member of the Council of the Tate in St Ives. He is a trustee of the Stowe House Preservation Trust and a member of its Interiors Working Group. He is currently Chairman of the educational charity Children in Crisis.

ANNABEL WESTMAN FSA is the Executive Director of The Attingham Trust for the study of historic houses and collections. She is an independent textile historian, consultant and writer specialising in the restoration of interiors for heritage bodies including the National Trust, English Heritage and Historic Royal Places. She is a trustee of the Stowe House Preservation Trust and a member of its Interiors Working Group.

Just like the building that it celebrates, this book is the work of many people and I am indebted to all our authors for recording their expertise, understanding and personal views of Stowe. The book owes much to Andy Marshall, whose photography captures so well the majesty of the building and the beauty of its decorative detail. The photography of Will Pryce and of the late Paul Barker has added to the richness of the photographic record, as has that of Anna McEvoy. I am grateful to them all for agreeing to the use of their images. Many of the historic images were sourced by Susannah Stone, whose help has been invaluable, along with the cooperation of Agata Rutkowska from the Royal Collection, Johanna Ward from Cambridge University Libraries, Jennifer Jeffrey at AKG Images and Stephanie Poynton of the National Trust.

The book would not have been possible without the hard work and patience of Linda Schofield, as project manager and copy editor, while the finished product is the result of the skills of the designer, Robert Dalrymple. It is impossible to enjoy Stowe House, whether it be from a passing view across the landscape garden or from a detailed architectural study, without marvelling at the creative vision of those who owned and built it, so it is appropriate first and foremost to acknowledge them for the extraordinary building that we celebrate here and that many of us are privileged to call our place of work. Today, however, we could not fully appreciate the importance of the house without the work of the many craftsmen and women who have been involved in the restoration that this book records. Their skills are truly breathtaking and the quality of their work will have ensured the survival of Stowe House as the centre of a seat of learning and heritage attraction.

Today, no visit to Stowe House would be complete without the care and attention of our volunteer team who present the building, recounting the stories of its owners and the artists who served them. Our volunteers are proud of the house and their work and we, in turn, are proud and very grateful to them for giving so freely of their time to ensure that a visit to Stowe is worthwhile, instructive and memorable. This book recognises and thanks them for all that they do.

Last, but by no means least, the book has been funded by World Monuments Fund, to whom, along with all our supporters and donors, I extend my very sincere thanks for their extraordinary generosity. Without funding from so many sources, including the visiting public, we could not have achieved our objective: the saving of a real architectural masterpiece.

N.S. MORRIS
Stowe, January 2018

Picture Credits

Front cover, back cover, pp. 8–9, 11, 12, 16, 20–21, 25, 26, 32, 36 (below), 38 (above), 39 (right), 40 (above right), 41, 42, 47, 48, 49 (below), 50–51, 52 (left above and below, and right above), 53, 55, 57, 58–59, 62, 63, 65, 70, 75, 77, 80 (above), 86 (below), 87, 88, 89 (right), 90 (centre and below), 92, 93, 98 (right), 101, 104, 108, 142: © Andy Marshall

Frontispiece, p. 67: Paul Barker / Country Life Picture Library

pp. 14, 17, 40 (centre and below), 43 (left), 44, 45, 52 (right below), 85 (left), 96 (above), 99 (left), 122: SHPT Archive

pp. 15, 35, 39 (left), 46 (below), 68–69, 100, 102–3: Anna McEvoy

p. 18 (left): Stephen Dorey – Bygone Images / Alamy Stock Photo

p. 18 (right): National Portrait Gallery, London

p. 19: Bruce White

p. 22: Hall Bequest Trust / SHPT

p. 23 (above): Sir John Soane Museum

p. 23 (below left): Ivan Vdovin / Alamy Stock Photo

p. 23 (below right): Ashmolean Museum, University of Oxford, UK / Bridgeman Images

pp. 24 (above), 28 (right above): Cambridge University Library

p. 24 (below): © National Trust Images / Matthew Antrobus

p. 27 (left): Gado Images / Alamy Stock Photo

p. 27 (right): akg-images / Bildarchiv Monheim

p. 28 (left): Tretyakov Gallery, Moscow, Russia / Bridgeman Images

pp. 28 (right below), 36 (above), 37 (above left), 38 (below), 40 (above left), 49 (above), 60–61, 72, 73, 74, 76, 95, 96 (below centre and right), 99 (right), 114, 125, 148: Nick Morris

pp. 29, 37 (above right), 78–79, 146: © National Trust Images

pp. 30–31: Will Pryce / Country Life / IPC+ Syndication

p. 34: Royal Commission for Historic Monuments

p. 37 (below): The Bodleian Library, Oxford

pp. 43 (right), 86 (above), 89 (left), 111: R. and H. Chapman Photographers, SHPT Archive

pp. 46 (above), 120, 123, 124, 129, 130, 131, 132, 133, 134–35, 136, 138, 139: © Stowe School Ltd

pp. 46 (centre), 56 (above): Royal Collection Trust / © Her Majesty Queen Elizabeth II 2018

pp. 54–55: Louis Sinclair

p. 56 (below): Photograph by J. Mudd, SHPT Archive

pp. 64, 150: Country Life Picture Library

pp. 66, 91: Will Pryce / Country Life Picture Library

pp. 80 (below), 81, 82, 83: Purcell Architects

p. 84: Patrick Baty

p. 85 (right): Yale Center for British Art

p. 90 (above): Reproduced by kind permission of the Warner Textile Archive

p. 94: Buckinghamshire County Museum

p. 96 (below left): World Monuments Fund

p. 97: Image courtesy of Sutton Vane Associates

p. 98 (left): Jackson Stops and Staff

pp. 105, 106, 107: Rupert Harris

pp. 110, 112, 113: Trevor Proudfoot, Cliveden Conservation

pp. 115, 116, 117, 118 (above), 119: Hirst Conservation

p. 118 (below): London Churches in Photographs

pp. 126, 128 (below): MICA Architects

p. 127: Royal Institute of British Architects

p. 128 (above): Stowe School Archive

p. 137: Stowe Enterprises Limited

pp. 140–41: Charlie Garment and Patrick Wilson, Stowe School Drone Club

Index

Illustrations are denoted by the use of *italics*.